More Oil Cans for the Collector

W. Clark Miller and Sabra Sonewald

Schiffer Publishing Ltd
4880 Lower Valley Road, Atglen, PA 19310 USA

Disclaimer

The text, antique photographs, and products pictured in this book are from the collection of the authors of this book. It is not sponsored, endorsed, or otherwise affiliated with any of the companies whose products are represented herein. This book was derived from the author's independent research. No photographs in this book may be reproduced without the written permission of the authors.

Library of Congress Control Number: 2002114576

Designed by Mark David Bowyer
Type set in Americana XBd BT / Korinna BT

ISBN: 0-7643-1732-6
Printed in China
1 2 3 4

Published by Schiffer Publishing Ltd.
4880 Lower Valley Road
Atglen, PA 19310
Phone: (610) 593-1777; Fax: (610) 593-2002
E-mail: Schifferbk@aol.com
Please visit our web site catalog at **www.schifferbooks.com**
We are always looking for people to write books on new and related subjects. If you have an idea for a book, please contact us at the above address.

This book may be purchased from the publisher.
Include $3.95 for shipping.
Please try your bookstore first.
You may write for a free catalog.

In Europe, Schiffer books are distributed by
Bushwood Books
6 Marksbury Avenue
Kew Gardens
Surrey TW9 4JF England
Phone: 44 (0) 20 8392 8585
Fax: 44 (0) 20 8392 9876
E-mail: Bushwd@aol.com
Free postage in the UK. Europe: air mail at cost.

Dedication

We would like to dedicate this book to the Henry Ford Museum & Greenfield Village in Dearborn, Michigan. As donors to the museum for years, we praise their dedication to the preservation of authentic automotive, oil, gas, and related historical items. From an original Texaco one-bay station acquired one day before demolition to a 1934 Texaco air flow tanker truck and pump island, from a Conoco filling station, to a Polarine tank wagon, and diner—they have it all. We urge all who collect petrolania or railroad memorabilia, and other transportation enthusiasts to visit. It is fun and educational for young and old alike. We simply cannot say enough good things about the museum and its dedication to this subject we truly love.

As an added bonus while in Dearborn, Michigan, cruise down Michigan Avenue and visit the original 1930s Amoco Service Station still in use today. They'll let you take all the photos you want.

Acknowledgments

The authors would like to acknowledge the following people for their help over the years in building our collection. Mr. Scott Benjamin, Mr. Norm Griffin, Wayne Henderson, Ed Love, Mr. J. Sam McIntyre, Jeff and Ellen Wood, Bill and Carla Sigsworth, Tom and Char Whitlatch, Charles Whitworth, Pat Quail, Ed Copelin, Ron Bettin, and my fellow collectors.

A special thanks to Mike Axel at Axel Photography. Also thanks to Sabra Sonewald for her help and encouragement.

Contents

Introduction

I have been interested in Petrolania collecting since I was about five years old. When my mother stopped at local gas stations I would collect cans, maps and other small items that were available there. I guess it was the graphics and all the different brands that appealed so much to me. I would even bug my mother to stop at service stations we never dealt with just to add cans to my collection. I still have about 100 of these cans in my collection. Sabra joined me five years ago and has helped greatly in expanding the collection. She continues to look for and find new items weekly.

Clark, my father, worked at Lubrizol Corporation in Wickliffe, Ohio, developing additives for oil and gasoline and other types of fuels and lubricants. He would bring home product cans with his additives in them. My father made many improvements to oil products that are still in use today. In his lifetime, he managed to amass forty-six patents for the industry.

I became interested again after going to an antique show and picking up a couple of items. What started as an interest is now a full-blown passion, with a collection of 20,000 + pieces of service station history!

In this book, we share our vast can collection with you—cans from A & P to Zeronis, dating from 1880-1980. We have tried to date each item as accurately as possible. In some cases exact dates can be determined. However, many oil companies did not date cans and the dates can only be approximated from the literature of the time period that the brand or logo was in use. We have also tried to determine the location of each of the oil companies represented here and have listed these in each companies heading. Other important information is included in each photo's caption.

The prices quoted are for estimation only as condition, rarity, and originality all have a direct effect on prices of these cans, as with collectibles in general. The grading guide is just that. A can considered to be in #9 condition to us may only be in #8 condition to someone else. We leave the final decision to you, the collector, and hope this book is a valuable addition to your library. Happy collecting.

Oil Can Grading

Grade 10

This is the best condition in which to find a can. This is most likely an unfilled display can with no surface scratches or rubbing from filling or shipping and no discoloration from oil, chemicals, or sun fade. Both tops and bottoms are bright on paper or plastic cans. There is no damage to labels. All original seals will be intact. Of the 10,000 cans in my collection, only about 50 fall into this classification.

Grade 9

This can has scratches or rubbing that would have to be looked for, and may have very minor sun fade.

Grade 8

Up to 10% of can, not normally on the face, may show light damage, including rubbing, scratches or sun fade.

Grade 7

This is the last grade in the excellent category. The can may show very heavy scratches, rubbing and fading or discoloration from oil or chemicals; top and bottom will show rust and discoloration.

Grade 6

More than 20%, but not over 40% of the surface will show scratches, rubbing, sun fade, and rust. The design will show and display well but may have pin holes in the top and bottom.

Grade 5

Same condition as Grade 6 but will have dents over less than 40% of the can. Pin hole rust on can face and body may be present.

Grade 4

More than 40% but not over 60% of the can will show scratches, rust, dents, sun fade, and discoloration. The face of the can is still displayable.

Grade 3
60% to 80% of the can will have heavy damage with severe rust holes; up to 40% of the can will have damage to top and face.

Grade 2
Will show enough color and detail to be put in the right group of cans by brand. Major rust and/or damage will be present.

Grade 1
This example is a filler until one in better shape comes along.

Grade 0
More than 90% damage throughout. This can may be kept if this is the only known example of this company or brand name.

Container Type Codes

Please note that not all of these codes are used in this book. Special thanks to Ed Love and Villa Publishing Syndicate for standardizing our hobby in the early years.

AL	Aluminum, thin walled cans, 1960s-1970s
CP	Composite paper/foil cans, 1945-1980s
CAR	Cardboard cans, WWII era, 1942-1945
CT	Cone top
GB	Glass bottle/jar
PB	Plastic bottles
PC	Plastic cans
RS	Rib steel
SS	Straight sided steel, 1930-1970
VRT	Vertical rectangle steel

Known Can Manufacturers

American Can Company
Boise-Cascade
Container Can Company
Crown Cork & Seal
Georgia-Pacific Corporation, Atlanta GA
Hardesty Can Company, Denver CO
National Can Company
Owens-Illinois
The Texas Company
Penn Plastic, Creighton PA
S.A.Y. Industries Inc., Leonminster MA
Spiro-PAC
St. Louis Can Company
Sonoco Products Company, Hartsville SC
Stone Container Company, Orlando FL
Weyerhaeuser Paper Company

Date Coding Tips

1947: Viscosity was listed only on can tops. No SAE destination.
1948: Series 2 classification by Caterpillar Tractor Company for diesel engines.
1952: ML, MM, MS, DG, DM, and viscosity added to cans with SAE grade.
1953: 10W30 motor oils introduced.
1955: Series 3 classification by Caterpillar Tractor Company for diesel engines.
1963-64: Zip code added to cans.
1973: Bar codes (UPC) introduced.
1943-July 1, 1963: A one or two digit number between the city and state in the address is the postal zone used from 1943 to July 1, 1963. Example, the Shellzone Anti-Freeze one quart can's title block reads New York 20 New York, San Francisco 6 California.

Note: The copyright date or patent numbers will also give an idea of time period during which a can was produced.

Cans With Open Dates

Amoco

This coding starts about 1953. The code will appear on the back of the can towards the bottom. This example is from a 1961 vintage Permalube 1 quart can.

262-24X-1q-FC-01/61

262: Brand name Permalube
24X: 24 cans to a case
1 qt: can size
FC: Not used for this purpose
01/61: Design first used January 1961

Atlantic

Any can listed as Atlantic Refining Company was produced before the Spring of 1966. Any can listing Atlantic Richfield was produced after the Spring of 1966.

BP

Any can listing Wilmington, Delaware dates 1969 and earlier; any listing Cleveland, Ohio is 1970 and on.

Deep Rock

Any Deep Rock can listing Kerr McGee is 1955 and on.

Esso

In July 1963, with the reformulation of all of its motor oil products, Humble Oil started using a code system on most of its product containers. The first letter is the division.

ESSO = S
HUMBLE = H
ENCO = N

The number after the letter is the product.

UNIFLO = 1
EXTRA = 2
MOTOR OIL = 3

The letter was added when the can design or formula was upgraded.

A, B, etc.

Example: S2B = Esso Extra

Gulf

This code applies to all Gulf products from 1950-1985. Disregard all the letters in the code except for the last three or four. The first is the month code and the second set is the year. The code is as listed below:

S P E C I A L T Y 0
1 2 3 4 5 6 7 8 9 0

Example from a Gulf Supreme 1 quart can:
C4E-S S - A 0
1 1 6 0 = 11/60

This can design was introduced in November of 1960.

Mobiloil

1930-1955: Socony Vacuum Oil Company
1955-1966: Socony-Mobil Oil Company
1966-On: Mobil Oil Corporation

Pure Oil

Most Pure Oil cans from 1949 have a date code that appears on the back of the can, sometimes on the bottom or about half way up on the right side. This code is for a 1960 High HP Purelube 1 quart can:

HPL-60-1

High HP Purelube, 1960, one quart. This design was introduced in 1960.

Spur

Cans dated 1/80-7/81 were made by Container Corporation of America.

Sunoco

From 1937 on, Sunoco cans are dated on the front or the back towards the bottom.

Texaco

All Texaco cans from 1954 carry an open date on the reverse side.

Example: 9/54

Reproduction Cans

The upsurge of the petrolania hobby has continued steadily over the past several years. Along with increased prices and demand, has come reproduction and/or fantasy items. They are currently available on Internet auction sites and through some trade and automotive magazines.

I personally think these reproduced and fantasy items hurt the hobby rather than promote it. Whenever I see a large number of reproduction items in an auction, I constantly question other items in that auction. Do they look too new? Do the items not match the roughness of other items in the collection? Whenever you suspect or get a gut feeling that something is wrong with the item, it is probably a reproduction. Trust your instincts and you won't get taken.

Here are a few things to observe about reproduction cans: (1) They look too new; (2) They have shiny tops that generally don't have oil weight stamped on them; (3) The seams look different than other cans of the same vintage; (4) The logo design doesn't match the product vintage; (5) Many appear to have a dull, flat finish.

Currently listed reproductions:

Blakely's 10-30 oil can
Hancock quart motor oil can
Blakely's quart motor oil can
Pure as Gold Pep Boys oil can
Gilmore Large Lion Head oil can
Clipper quart motor oil can
Husky Cody Wyoming oil can
Polly Prem quart oil can
Pathfinder quart oil can
Sunset Penn quart oil can
Skunk Oil quart motor oil can
Phillips Trop-Artic oil can
Power Lube quart oil can
Indian motorcycle oil can
Gilmore Lion Head oil can
Mohawk quart oil can
Hudson motor oil quart can
Strata motor oil quart can
Jayhawk quart oil can
Skyway quart motor oil can
Air Race motor oil can
Clipper Aviation oil can
Penn Franklin quart oil can

Directory of Cans

American Cans

A & P
Atlantic & Pacific Tea Co.

A&P All Season, 1961 (SS) one-quart can. $20-$40.

A Penn, Division Penn Corp.
Butler, PA

A Penn Dry Cleaner, 1941 (SS) one-gallon can. $40-$60.

A Penn 10W30, 1961 (SS) one-quart can. $20-$30.

A Penn Dry Cleaner (Reverse Side)

A Small Injun Product
Indianapolis, IN

Small Injun Tune Up, 1962 (SS) 8-oz. can with paper label. $20-$30.

Ajax Motor Oil

Ajax Motor Oil, 1940 (SS) one-quart can. $45-$75.

American Honda Motor Co.
Glendale, CA

Honda Two Stroke Motorcycle Injector Oil, 1975 (CP) one-quart. $15-$25.

Action Industries
Kansas City, KS

AP ATF, 1970 (CP) one-quart can. $15-$25.

American Fuel & Supply Co. Inc.
Milwaukee, WI

AFSCO Outboard, 1966 (CP) one-quart can. $20-$35.

American Oil Co.

Penn AMO, 1938 (SS) one-quart can. $45-$65.

American Petrofina
Dallas, TX

Fina Outboard, 1961 (SS) one-quart can.
$30-$40.

Amoco/Standard Oil of Indiana
Chicago, IL

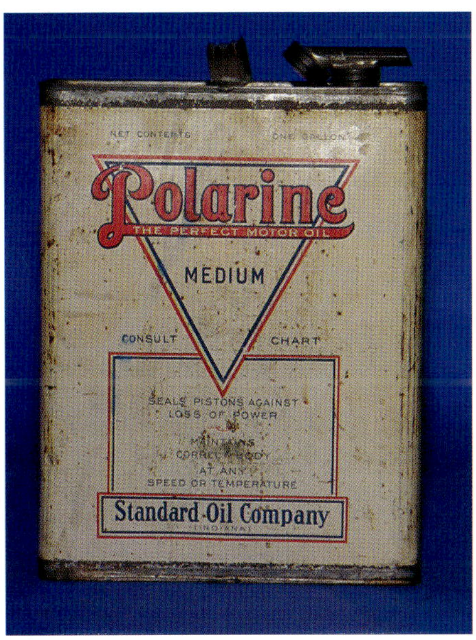

Polarine Motor Oil Medium, 1931 (SS) one-gallon can. $150-$250.

Polarine Type "F" Motor Oil, 1931 (SS) one-gallon metal can with paper label.
$150-$250.

Polarine "F" for Fords, 1929 (SS) two-quart can. 2 variations.
$75-$125 each.

Polarine, 1915 (SS) two-quart can. $675-$1200.

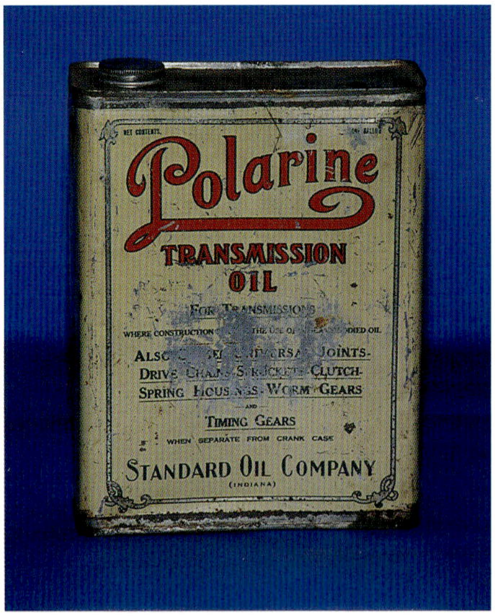

Polarine Transmission Oil, 1929 (SS) one-gallon can. $125-$225.

Polarine Fibre Grease, 1925 (SS) 10-pound can. $125-$175.

Polarine Cup Grease, Left 1929 (SS) five-pound can; Right 1931 (SS) five-pound can. $50-$75.

Polarine Cup Grease, 1930 (SS) one-pound can. $40-$60.

Polarine Pressure-Gun Grease, 1925 (SS) one-pound can. $50-$75.

Eureka Belt Dressing, 1910 (SS) one-gallon can. $75-$125.

Stanolind Liquid Paraffin, 1929 (SS), one-gallon can. $75-$125.

Amoco Permalube, 1943 (GB) one-gallon with paper label. $60-$90.

Semdac Liquid Gloss, 1941 (SS) one-quart can. $40-$60.

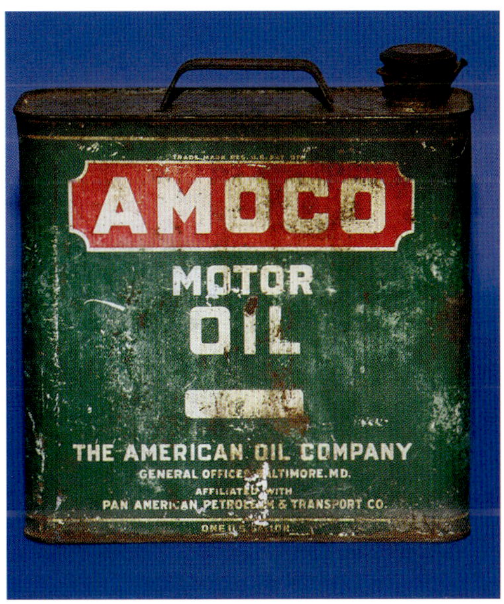

Amoco Motor Oil, 1925 (SS) one-gallon can. $75-$150.

Standard Permalube, 8/59 (SS) one-quart can. Rare silver variation. $30-$60.

Permalube Motor Oil, 1961 (SS) five-quart can. $30-$40.

Amoco Super Anti-Freeze, 1956 (SS) one-gallon can. Also sold in one-quart can. $30-$50.

American Outboard, 01/61 (SS) one-pint can. $20-$30.

Standard Oil Indiana Dealer Special, 1956 (SS) two-gallon can. $25-$45.
These were given to the dealers at no charge with purchase of Stanolind two-gallons.

Standard Aviation Engine Oil, 1955 (SS) one-gallon can. $250-$350.

Amoco Home Oil, 1940 (SS) 4-oz. $25-$35.

Finol Household Oil, Left: 1925 (SS) 4-oz.; Middle: 1943 (GB) 4-oz.; Right: 1948 (SS) 4-oz. $35-$125 each.

Standard Grease Salesman Sample, 11/53 (SS), one-pound can, $40-$60; Amoco Grease, 1940 (SS) one-pound can, $25-$35; Standard Cup, 1950 (SS) one-pound can, $40-$60.

Finol/Pan Am Household Oil, Left to right: 1949 (SS) 4-oz. (variation), 12/51 (SS) 4-oz.; 4/57 (SS) 4-oz.; 1/61 (SS) 4-oz.; 3/65 (SS) 4-oz.; 6/68 (SS) 4-oz.
$30-$40 each.

Amoco Standard Grease, Top: 4/59 (SS) one-pound can; Left: 01/61 (SS) one-pound can; Right: 01/61 (SS) one-pound can. $25-$35

Standard/Solite/Amolite Lighter Fluid, Left to right: 10/53 (SS) 4-oz.; 7/62 (SS) 4-oz.; 6/65 (SS) 4-oz.; 6/68 (SS) 4-oz. sold at American Stations; 6/68 (SS) 4-oz. sold at Standard Stations. $20-$35 each.

Amoco Stanolind, 4/52 (SS) one-pound can, $25-$45; Amoco Jell, 01/61 (SS) one-pound can. $15-$30

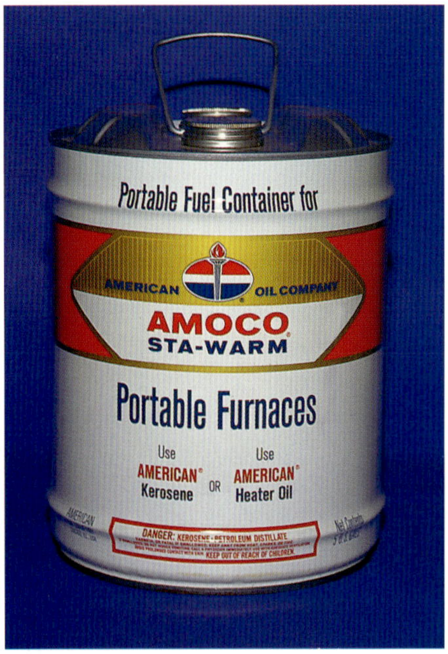

Amoco Sta-Warm, 1967 (SS) five-gallon fuel can, $50-$85. This can was sent to buyers of Amoco portable furnaces for fuel oil purchases.

Utoco Motor Oil, 1955 (SS) five-gallon can. $50-$100.

Amoco S.O. Charcoal Starter, Amoco Insect Killer, Left: 12/64, one-quart can; Right: 9/66, 14-oz. $15-$30 each.

Vico Household Oil, 1935 (SS) 4-oz. $225-$325.

Utah Oil & Ref. Co., Utoco 10W30, 1954 (SS) one-quart can.
$75-$125

Anderson Prichard Oil Corp.
Oklahoma City, OK

Challenge XS, 1950 (SS) one-quart can. $30-$50.

Apex Oil Products
Minneapolis, MN

Penntrol, 1941 (SS) one-quart can. $85-$125.

Archer Petro Co.
Omaha, NE

Archer Lubricants Chief Aircraft, 1960 (SS) one-quart can. $35-$45.

Archer Lubricants Ford ATF Type "F", 1963 (SS) one-quart can. $30-$40.

Archer Lubricants Non Additive Type, 1970 (CP) one-quart can. $25-$35.

Arlans Department Stores
New York, NY

Arlans Motor Oil, 1973 (CP) one-quart can. $15-$25.

Arnold Dist. Co.
Texarkana, TX; N. Little Rock, AK; Denver, CO

Road Runner Motor Oil, 1970 (CP) one-quart can; Road Runner Motor Oil, 1975 (CP) one-quart can. $40-$60 each.

Ashland Oil Co.
Ashland, KY

Minamax Motor Oil, 1958 (SS) one-quart can. $25-$35.

Ashland Oil Products, 1963 (SS) five-gallon can. $30-$50.

Associated Oil Co.; Tidewater Oil Co.

New York, NY; San Francisco, CA

Veedol Heavy #3, 1925 (SS) one-gallon can. $75-$125.

Veedol Motor Oil, 1956 (SS) one-quart can. $25-$45.

Veedol Marine, 1947 (SS) one-quart can. $250-$350.

Cycol Lubricating Grease, 1929 (SS) 10-pound can. Value not estimable.

Tydol HD, 1947 (SS) one-quart can. $50-$75; Veedol HD Plus, 1956 (SS) one-quart can. $25-$45.

Veedol Outboard, Left: 1959 (SS) one-quart can; Right: 1962 (PB) one-quart can. $25-$35.

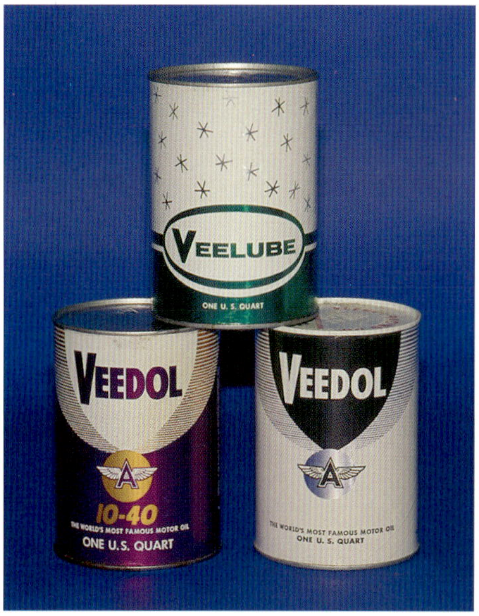

Veelube, 1971 (CP) one-quart can; Veedol 10W40 (1972) (CP) one-quart can; Veedol Racing Oil, 1971 (CP) one-quart can. $20-$35 each.

Veedol All Purpose Grease, 1955 (SS) one-pound can. $30-40.

Veedol Medium Cup, 1961 (SS) one-pound can. $20-$30.

Atlantic Coast Oil Co. of New York
Glendale, NY

Pennoco Motor Oil, 1938 (SS) one-quart can. $60-$85.

Atlantic/Richfield
Philadelphia, PA; Los Angeles, CA

Atlantic Motor Oil Polarine, 1925 (SS) one-gallon can. $125-$225.

Atlantic Capitol, 1929 (SS) one-gallon can. $125-$200.

Atlantic Quality, 1950 (SS) one-quart can. $25-$35.

Atlantic Motor Oil, 1930 (SS) one-gallon can. $75-$125.

Atlantic Capitol Motor Oil, Left: 1947 (SS) two-gallon can; Right: 1960 (SS) two-gallon can. $30-$40 each.

Atlantic Aviation Motor Oil, 1960 (SS) one-quart can. $25-35.

Atlantic Motorboat Oil, 1957 (SS) one-quart can. $175-$350 (Rare).

Atlantic Motor Cup Grease, 1930 (SS) five-pound can. $60-$80.

Richfield Pennsylvania, 1955 (SS) one-quart can; Richfield ATF, 1958 (SS)
one-quart can. $50-$75 each.

Atlantic Grease, Left: 1940 (SS) one-pound can; Right: 1960 (SS) one-pound can. $25-$45.

Richfield Outboard Motor Oil, 1956 (SS) one-quart can. $50-$75.

Richfield Pennsylvania Motor Oil, 1948 (SS) one-quart can. $75-$175.
Richfield Motor Oil, 1961 (SS) one-quart can. $50-$75.

Richfield Outboard Motor Oil, 1963 (SS) one-quart can. $45-$65.

Rocor Motor Oil, 1961 (SS) two-gallon can.
$25-$35.

Assorted Richfield Car Care Products; all 1960 (SS) 12 oz./8 oz. cans.
$20 -$30 each.

Autolene Oil Co.
Baltimore, MD

Rocor Motor Oil, 1949 (SS) two-gallon can.
$35-$45.

Autolene XP, 1949 (SS) one-quart can.
$20-$50.

Richlube Lithium, 1961 (SS) one-pound can. $25-$35.

Autolene XP, 1969 (CP) one-quart can. $20-$50.

Avia Motor Oil

Avia Motor Oil, 1940 (SS) one-quart can. $40-$60.

Bradford Oil Refining Co.
Bradford, PA

Allpen Motor Oil, 1946 (SS) one-quart can. $150-$250. Permit #10.

Bodic Hoover Petro Co.
Chicago, IL; Warren, PA

Sta Cool Outboard Motor Oil, 1961 (SS) one-quart can. $35-$55.

Pennstate Heavy Duty, 1957 (SS) one-quart can. $30-$60.

Brooks Oil Co.
Cleveland, OH

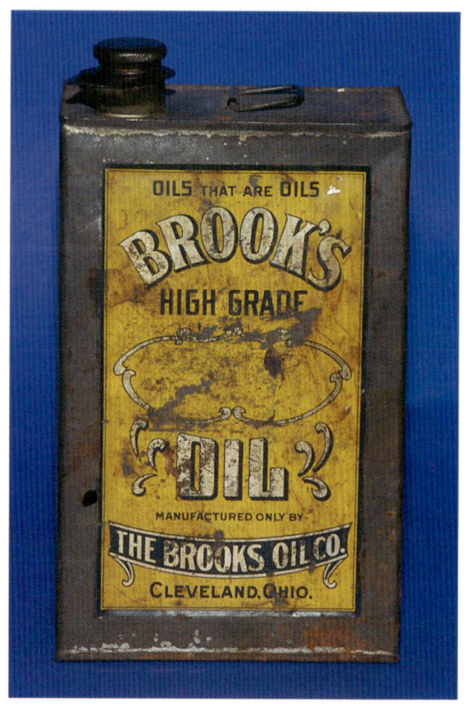

Brooks High Grade, 1920 (SS) one-gallon can. $75-$125.

CA-MOR Inc.
Indianapolis, IN

Empire State, 1969 (CP) one-quart can. $25-$35.

Canfield Oil Co.
Canfield, OH

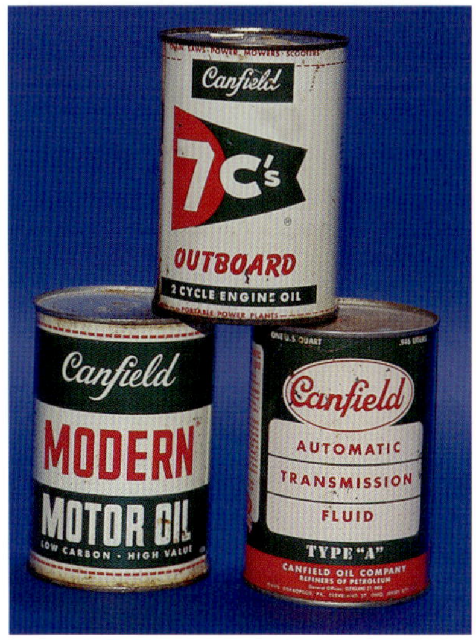

Canfield Can Assortment, 1963 (SS) one-quart cans. $35-$125 each.

William Penn Oil Cans, All 1970 (SS) one-quart cans. $20-$35 each.

Wm. Penn Motor Oil, 1953 (SS) five-gallon can. $25-$45.

100% Pure Pennsylvania, Left: 1934 (SS) five-gallon can; Right: 1934 (SS) two-gallon can. $40-$75 each.

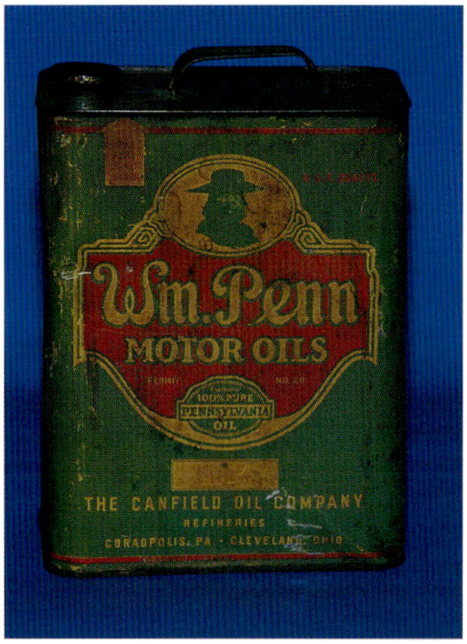

Wm. Penn Motor Oils, 1935 (SS) two-gallon can. $45-$65.

Canfield 2 Cycle Engine Oil, 1961 (SS) 8 oz. can. $15-$20.

Wm. Penn Valve Ease, 1943 (GB) one-pint. $25-$35.

Carquest Corp.
Packaged by Ashland Oil Co.
Terrytown, NY

Carquest Motor Oil, 1975 (CP) one-quart can. $10-$20.

Cato Oil & Grease Co.
Oklahoma City, OK

Wanda Motor Oil, Top: 1960 (SS); Left: 1960 (SS); Right: 1963 (RS), quarts. $25-$35 each.

PENNtroleum, 1963 (SS) one-quart can. $25-$35.

Merit Motor Oil, 1957 (SS) one-quart can. $60-$110.

Merit Motor Oil, 1970 (CP) one-quart can. $20-$25.

Century-Morrison Co.
Dallas, TX

Texas Star, 1958 (SS) one-quart can. $50-$75.

Champlin Oil Co.
Enid, OK

Champlin Deluxe, 1945 (SS) one-quart can. $30-$40.

Cen-Pe-Co

Cen-Pe-Co Super Refined, 1967 (SS) one-quart can. No company name. $25-$35.

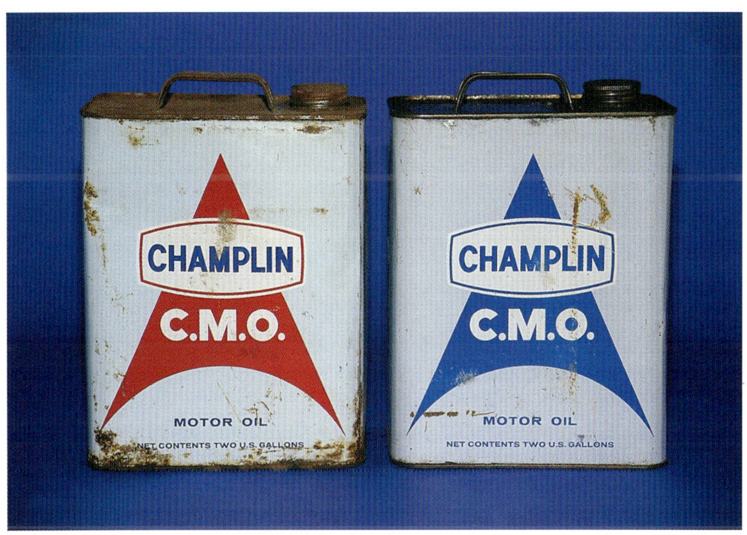

Champlin CMO, Left: 1963 two-gallon can; Right: 1969 two-gallon can. $25-$40 each.

H and H Special, 1946 (SS) two-gallon can. $40-$60.

Chemical Research Laboratories

Stabl Flo Oil Additive, 1956 (SS) one-quart can. $50-$75.

Chevron; Standard Oil of California
San Francisco, CA

Zerolene for Fords, 1925 (SS) one-gallon can. $250-$350.

Zerolene Transmission Lubricant, 1925 (SS) 10 pound can. $40-$60.

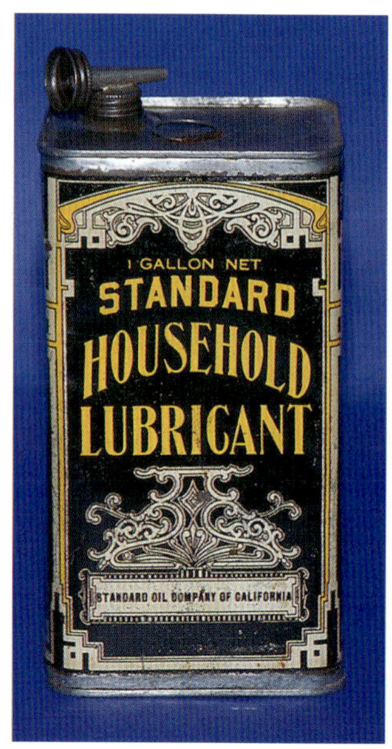

Standard Household Lubricant, 1920 (SS) one-gallon can. $175-$275.

Zerolene Valve Oil, 1929 (SS) one-quart can. $75-$125.

Hand Separator Oil, 1930 (SS) one-gallon can. $75-$100

RPM Aviation Oil, 1969 (CP) one-quart can. $25-$35.

RPM ATF Dextron, 1966 (CP) one-quart can. $25-$35.

RPM ATF Dextron, 1969 (SS) one-pint can. RPM Outboard Super RCD, 1969 (SS) one-pint can. $20-$30 each.

Chevron RPM five-gallon product can (Delo Special) 1955 (SS). $25-$45.

RPM Type "A" Western Division, 1951 (SS) one-quart can. $25-$35

RPM New Blue Outboard, 1965 (SS) 6 oz. can. $20-$30.

RPM 2 Cycle Oil, 1964 (PB) one-quart can; RPM Outboard Oil, 1965 (PB) one-quart can. $20-$30 each.

RPM Handy Oil, 1947 (SS) 4-oz.; Esco Handy Oil, 1955 (SS) 4-oz.; Chevron Handy Oil, 1959 (SS) 4-oz. $25-$35.

RPM Handy Oil, Left: 1969 (SS) 4-oz.; Right: 1965 (SS) 4-oz.; Chevron Lighter Fluid, 1965 (SS) 4-oz. $25-$35.

RPM Grease, Left: 1945 (SS) one-pound can; Middle: 1950 (SS) one-pound can; Right: 1957 (SS) one-pound can. $20-$40 each.

Standard Thinner No. 350, 1963 (SS) one-gallon can. $30-$40.

Christenson Oil Co., Portland or Distributors

Portland, OR

Aero Motor Oil, 1958 (SS) one-quart can. $75-$150.

Chrysler Corporation
Parts Division
Detroit, MI

Mopar Supreme, 1972 (CP) one-quart can. $30-$50.

Max Motor Oil, 1976 (CP) one-quart can. $15-$25.

Cities Service/Citgo
Tulsa, OK

Cities Service Motor Oil, 1925 (SS) one-quart can. $50-$75.

Cities Service Oils, 1930 (SS) one-gallon can. $40-$60

Trojan Motor Oil, Left: 1955 (SS) one-quart can; Right: 1957 (SS) one-quart can. $30-$45.

Cities Service Triple HD Koolmotor, 1963 (CP) one-quart can. $25-$35; Cities Service C Series, 1963 (SS) one-quart can. $25-$35.

Cities Service Permanent Anti-Freeze, 1948 (SS) one-gallon can. $75-$125.

Cities Service HD Koolmotor, 1961 (SS) one-gallon can. $30-$40.

Cities Service Outboard, Left: 1950 (SS) one-pint can; Right: 1955 (SS) one-pint can. $15-$25.

Cities Service Premium Anti-Freeze, 1957 (SS) one-quart can. $75-$125.

Cities Service Outboard, 1963 (SS) one-pint can; Cities Service Koolmotor Outboard, 1963 (SS) one-pint can. $15-$25 each.

Cities Service Outboard Gear Oil, 1953 (SS) one-quart can. $40-$60.

Cities Service, Left to Right: 1949 (SS) 4 oz.; 1954 (SS) 4 oz.; 1950 (SS) 4 oz.; 1956 (SS) 4 oz. $25-$75 each.

Utility Oil, 1939 (SS) 4 oz.; Penetrating Oil, 1939 (SS) 4 oz. $30-$45 each.

Cities Service, Left to Right: 1963 (SS) 4 oz.; 1963 (SS) 4 oz.; 1963 (SS) 4 oz. $25-$35.

Trojan Grease, Left: 1945 (SS) one-pound can; Middle: 1953 (SS) one-pound can; Right: 1957 (SS) one-pound can. $25-$40 each.

Trojan Grease, 1961 (SS) five-pound can. $20-$30.

Cities Service Product Can, 1962 (SS) one-gallon can. $20-$30.

Citgo C Series, Left: 1966 (CP) one-quart can; Right: 1971 (CP) one-quart can. $25-$35.

Cities Service Cisco Solvent, Left: 1946 (SS) five-quart can; Right: 1952 (SS) five-quart can. $40-$60.

Citgo Outboard, 1966 (CP) one-quart can. $50-$85.

Cisco Pep, 1950 (SS) 4 oz.; Engine Pep, 1955 (SS) 4 oz. $10-$20 each.

Citgo Premium Anti-Freeze, 1966 (SS) one-quart can. $25-$35.

Clark Oil & Refining Co.
Milwaukee, WI

Clark Anti-Freeze and Summer Coolant, 1969 (SS) one-quart can. $45-$75.

Colorado Petroleum Co.
Denver, CO

Silver State Motor Oil, 1965 (CP) one-quart can. $20-$30.

Columbia Bedford
Kearny, NJ

Columbia Outboard and Lawn Mower, 1969 (CP) one-quart can. $20-$30.

Conoco
Ponca City, OK

Conoco Outboard, 1966 (PB) one-quart can. $15-$25.

Conoco Outboard, Left: 1957 (SS) one-pint can; Middle: 1963 (SS) 1-pint can; Right: 1966 (SS) one-pint can. $25-$35.

Conoco Grease, Top: 1945 (SS) one-pound can; Left: 1954 (SS) one-pound can; Right: 1954 (SS) one-pound can. $25-$45 each.

Conoco Super Lube, 1956 (SS) five-pound can. $25-$35.

Conoco Grease, Top: 1940 (SS) one pound can; Left: 1945 (SS) one-pound can; Right: 1947 (SS) one-pound can. $25-$45 each.

Conoco Grease, all 1957 (SS) one-pound cans. $25-$125. Axle is rare.

Conoco Pressure Lube Grease, 1960 (SS) five-pound can. $25-$35.

Conoco Grease, Top: 1948 (SS) one-pound can; Left: 1950 (SS) one-pound can; Right: 1950 (SS) one-pound can. $25-$45 each.

Conoco Grease Cans, all 1966 (SS) one-pound cans. $25-$35.

Conoco Lubequik Power Chassis Lubricant, 1948 (SS) 8 oz. can. $40-$60.

Conoco Anti-Squeak Oil, 1945 (SS) one-gallon can. $35-$65.

Conoco Tunes It, 1955 (SS) one-pint can. $20-$30. Rare

Conoco Anti-Squeak Household Oil, 1936 (SS) 4-oz. $125-$225.

Consumers Co-Operative Assoc.
Kansas City, KS

CO-OP 4 Cycle Motorcycle Oil, 1969 (CP) one-quart can. $40-$60.

Natural & LP Gas, 1960 (SS) one-quart can. $40-$60. Premium & Super TMS, 1980 (CP) one-quart can. $15-$25.

Top: CO-OP Motor Oil, 1958 (SS); Left: CO-OP Motor Oil, 1962 (SS) one-quart can; Right: CO-OP Motor Oil, 1958 (SS), one-quart can. $30-$50.

CO-OP ATF, 1961 (SS) one-quart can. $35-$45.

Assorted CO-OP cans. All 1969 (CP) one-quart cans. $20-$30 each.

Continental Refining Co.
Oil City, PA

Coreco Penn, 1948 (SS) one-quart can. $65-$95.

Coreco Lube Motor Oil, 1950 (SS) two-gallon can. $40-$70.

L. L. Coryell & Sons
Lincoln, NE

Coryell 70 Super Motor Oil, 1938 (SS) one-quart can. $75-$100.

Cosden Oil and Refining
Big Spring, TX

Cosden Heavy Duty, Left: 1959 (SS) one-quart can; Right: 1963 (SS) one-quart can. $50-$75.

Cosden S-3, 1962 (SS) one-quart can. $30-$40.

Crew Levick
Delaware

Empire Non Carbon Heavy, 1920s (SS) 1/2-gal. can. No estimate.

Empire; note Cities Service style logo in corners.

Crown Central Petroleum Co.
Baltimore, MD; Houston, TX; New York, NY

Greenzoil, 1940 (SS) one-quart can. $45-$75.

Crown Premium Motor Oil, 1963 (SS) one-quart can. $40-$60.

Crown ATF, 1973 (CP) one-quart can. $20-$30.

Cruiser Motor Oil

Cruiser Motor Oil, 1939 (SS) two-gallon can. $75-$125.

Dato Service/Supply
Park Ridge, IL

Oil State All Weather, 1975 (CP) one-quart can. $20-$30.

Custer City Oil Co.
Bradford, PA

Preferred Penn, 1950 (SS) one-quart can. $45-$65.

Davis Refining Co.
Tallahassee, FL

Top-Kik Motor Oil, 1975 (CP) one-quart can. $15-$25. Britelube Motor Oil, 1975 (CP) one-quart can. $15-$25.

Deep Rock Refining
Richmond, VA

Rocklube Motor Oil, 1960 (SS) one-quart can. $40-$60.

Deep Rock/Kerr-McGee
Chicago, IL

Valve Lube, 1971 (CP) one-quart can. $15-$25.

Deep Rock Prize Water Pump, 1954 (SS) one-pound can. $20-$30.

Deep Rock, Left: 1957 (SS) two-gallon can; Right: 1960 (SS) two-gallon can. $25-$35.

Kerr McGee Household Oil, 1965 (SS) 4 oz. $30-$40.

Deep Valley Oil Co.
Barberton, OH

Bulkway Motor Oil, 1947 (SS) two-gallon can. $35-$50. Trailway Motor Oil, 1961 (SS) two-gallon can. $20-$30.

Denver Oil Co.
Oklahoma City, OK

Denoco ATF Type A, 1966 (CP) one-quart can. $15-$25.

Dependable

Dependable Washing Machine Oil for use in gear cases; 1940 (SS) one-quart can. $35-$45.

Dependable Washing Machine Grease, 1940 (SS) one-pound can. $40-$60.

Derby
Wichita, KS

Derby Lighter Fluid, 1963 (SS) 4 oz. $25-$35.

Derby Oil Co. All 1972 (CP) one-quart cans. $20-$30.

Double Eagle Lubricants, Inc.
Oklahoma City, OK

Golden West Motor Oil, 1965 (CP) one-quart can. $ 25-$45. Double Eagle Motor Oil, 1947 (SS) one-quart can. $40-$60.

Crest Motor Oil, 1972 (CP) one-quart can. $15-$25.

Golden West Motor Oil, 1963 (RS) one-quart can; 1960 (SS) one-quart can. $225-$325 each.

Sup-R-Lub Motor Oil, 1973 (CP) one-quart can. $15-$25.

Double Eagle Motor Oil, 1980 (PC) one-quart can. $30-$40.

Drydene Oil Co.
Baltimore, MD; Warminster, PA; Orlando, FL

Drydene Motor Oil, 1979 (CP), one-quart can. $15-$25 each.

Dryer, Clark, Dryer Oil Co.,
Oklahoma City, OK

Mother Penn, Left: 1963 (SS) one-quart can; Right: 1969 (CP) one-quart can. $40-$60 each.

DX Sunray - Mid Continent Petroleum Co.
Tulsa, OK

Faultless Motor Oil, 1938 (SS) one-quart can. $125-$200.

DX Outboard, Left: 1963 (PB) one-quart can; Right: 1969 (PB) one-quart can. $25-$35.

DX Boron Extra Heavy Duty, Left: 1966 (CP) one-quart can; Right: 1970 (CP) one-quart can. $15-$30.

DX Household Oil, 1955 (SS) 4-oz. $40-$60. None known with new DX logo.

DX Ultra Special, 1970 (CP) one-quart can; DX ATF, 1970 (CP) one-quart can. $15-$25 each.

DX All Purpose Grease, 1950 (SS) one-pound can. $25-$35.

DX All Purpose Grease/Lubricant, Left: 1963 (SS) 5-pound can; Middle: 1966 (SS) 10-pound can; Right: 1969 (SS) 5-pound can. $25-$35 each.

El Paso Natural Gas Company
El Paso, TX

El Paso Extra Heavy Duty, 1964 (CP) one-quart can. $20-$30.

Electric Refining Company
Toledo, OH

The Electric Refining Co., 1935 (SS) five-gallon can. $50-$75.

Elk Refining Company
Charleston, WV

Elk Motor Oil, 1961 (SS) one-quart can. $25-$35.

Famous Lubricants Co.
Chicago, IL

Motor Life Oil, 1960 (SS) one-quart can. $30-$40.

Farmers Union Central Exchange
St. Paul, MN

CO-OP Premium Motor Oils (Top stamped Econex Non Det.) 1965 (SS) one-quart can. $25-$45.

Ford Motor Company
Dearborn, MI

Ford Genuine Anti-Freeze, 1935 (SS) one-quart can. Rare in one-quart size. $150-$250.

Fina Oil and Chemical Company
Dallas, TX

Fina ATF, Fina ATF, Fina Ultra Supreme, Fina HD Premium, Fina Shield, 1970s (CP) one-quart cans. $15-$25 each.

Rotunda 6000 Mile Motor Oil, Left: 1960 (SS) one-quart can; Center: 1961 (SS) five-quart can; Right: 1961 (SS) one-quart can. $40-$75 each.

Fina Lubricants, Left: 1956 (SS) one-pound can; Right: 1960 (SS) one-pound can. $15-$30 each.

Ford Rotunda 6000 Mile Motor Oil, five-quart can. (Reverse side).

Ford Rust Inhibitor, 1940 (SS) 8-oz. can. $40-$60.

Left: Ford Super Premium, 1972 (CP) one-quart can; Middle: Ford Premium Motor Oil, 1975 (CP) one-quart can and Motorcraft Super Duty, 1981 (CP) one-quart can; Right: Motor Craft Super Duty, 1981 (CP) one-quart can. $25-$35 each.

Ford Tractor Hydraulic Oil, Left: 1965 (SS) one-quart can; Right: 1965 (SS) one-gallon can. $30-$40.

Motor Craft Super Duty, 1975 (CP) one-quart can. $20-$30.

Ford Cooling System Cleaner, 1948 (SS). $15-$25.

Frantz Washing Machine Oil

Frantz Washing Machine Oil, 1945 (SS) one-quart can. $75-$125.

Gards Corp.
Kansas City, KS

Gard's Motor Oil, 1970 (CP) one-quart can. $15-$20.

General Motors
All Divisions
Detroit, MI

GM Polishing Cloth, 1948 (SS) one cloth. $15-$25.

Gamble-Skogmo Inc.
Minneapolis, MN

Varcon Liqui-matic, Left: 1956 (SS) one-quart can; Right: 1961 (SS) one-quart can. $20-$40.

General Motors
Buick Motors Division
Flint, MI

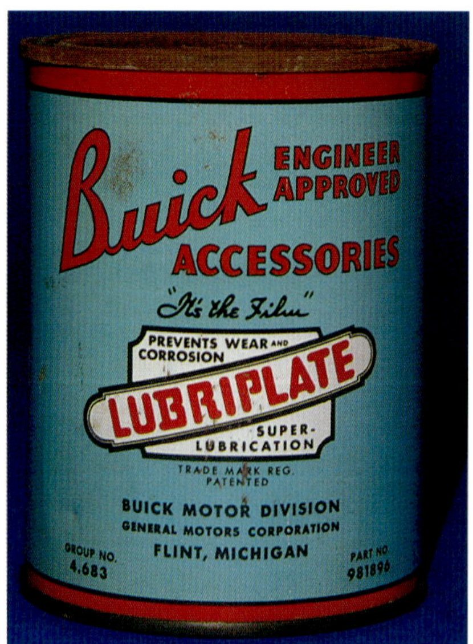

Buick accessories made by Lubriplate, 1947 (SS) one-pound can. $40-$60.

Buick Special Oil for Automatic Transmissions Type A Fluid, 3/62 (SS) one-quart can. $45-$75.

General Motors
Cadillac Division
Detroit, MI

Cadillac Hydra-matic Transmission Fluid, 1958 (SS) 5-quart can. $50-$125.

General Motors
Parts Division
Detroit, MI

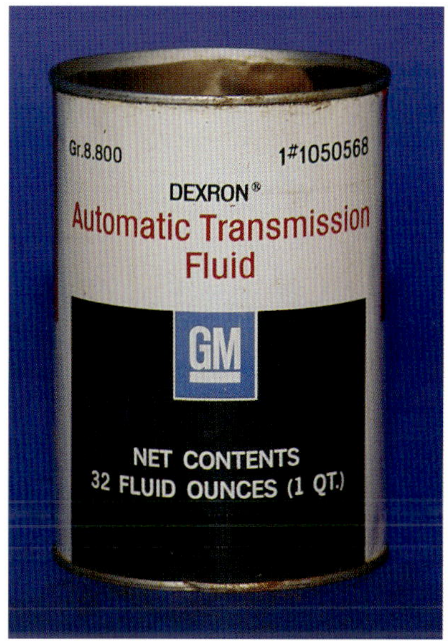

Dexron GM ATF, 11/68 (SS) one-quart can. $30-$40.

General Motors
Oldsmobile Division
Lansing, MI

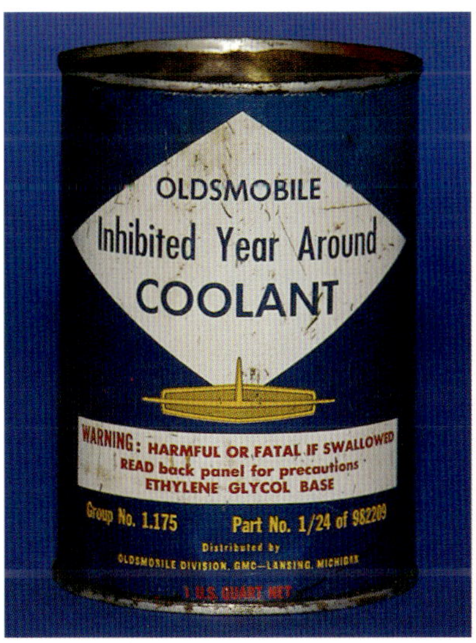

Oldsmobile Coolant, 1961 (SS) one-quart can. $40-$60.

GM Hydramatic Fluid, GM Anti-Freeze, 1956 (SS) one-quart cans. $40-$60.

Gibble Gas Company
Cushing, OK

Gibble Gas All Seasons, 1964 (CP) one-quart can. $20-$35.

Graham-Penn Oil Company
Houston; Dallas; Fort Worth, TX

Hi-Way Motor Oil, 1955 (SS) one-quart can. $75-$125.

GRC Company
Memphis, TN

Blue Diamond, 1973 (CP) one-quart can. Red Diamond, 1973 (CP) one-quart can. $20-$30.

Gulf Coast Lubricants Company
Houston, TX

Gulf Coast Regular, 1970 (CP) one-quart can. $10-$20.

Gulf Oil Corporation
Pittsburgh, PA

Gulf Supreme Auto Oil, 1920 (SS) one-gallon can. $75-$175.

Gulfpride Motor Oil, Left: 1948 (SS) one-quart can; Right: 1947 (SS) one-quart can. $45-$75 each.

Gulfpride Motor Oil, 5/63 (CP) one-quart can. $25-$45.

Gulfpride H.D., 1/57 (SS) one-quart can. $50-$75.

Gulfpride Single-G, Left: 1968 (CP) one-quart can; Right: 10/67 (CP) one-quart. $25-$35.

Gulfpride Super Premium 10W40, Left: 3/80 (PC) one-quart can; Right: 7/83 (CP) one-quart can. $15-$20.

Gulflube XHD, 6/58 (SS) one-quart can. $125-$175. Rare.

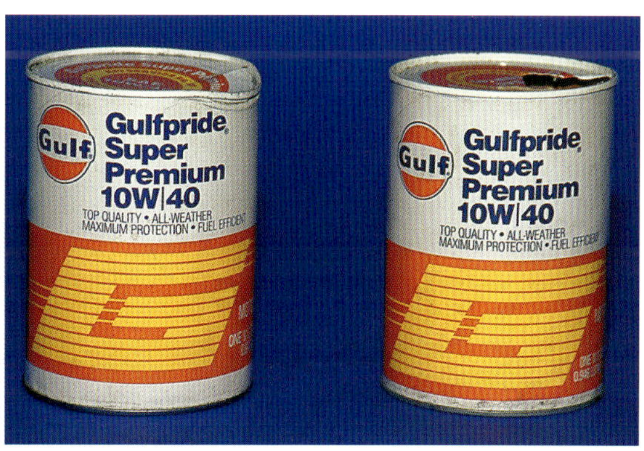

Gulfpride Premium 10W40, Left: 1/84 (PC) one-quart can; Right: 1/84 (CP) one-quart can. $15-$20.

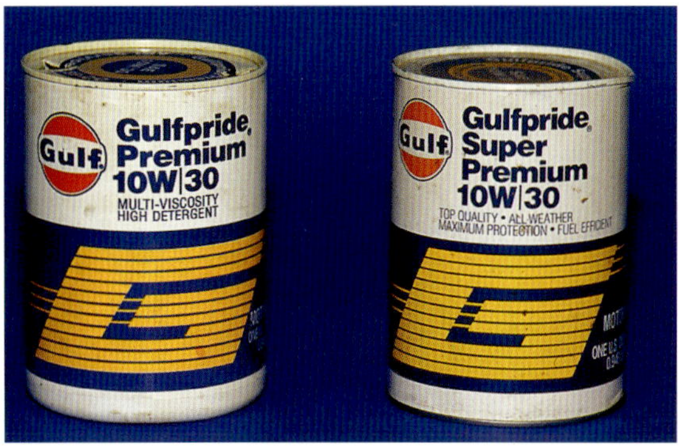

Gulfpride Super Premium 10W30, Left: 1/84 (PC) one-quart can; Right: 7/83 (CP) one-quart can. $15-$20.

Gulfpride Single-G, Left: 1/84 (PC) one-quart can; Right: 7/83 (CP) one-quart can. $15-$20.

Gulfpride, Top: 2/72 (PC) one-quart can; Center: 3/80 (PC) one-quart can; Right: 3/77 (PC) one-quart can. $25-$35.

Gulf Saphire, Top: 1/79 (CP) one-quart can; Left: 2/77 (PC) one-quart can; Right: 1/79 (PC) one-quart can. $20-$30.

Gulfpride Single, Top: 2/72 (CP) one-quart can; Left: 2/72 (PC) one-quart can; Right: 7/83 (CP) one-quart can. $25-$35.

Gulf Super G, 4/77 (SS) one-quart can; $150-$250. This is a very rare Gulf can to find. It is a synthetic oil test marketed in a limited area and did not sell and was dropped from product line.

Gulflube HD, Left: 1/75 (PC) one-quart can; Right: 1/75 (CP) one-quart can. $15-$30.

Gulf Super Duty Plus, Left: 1/81 (PC) one-quart can; Right: 7/83 (CP) one-quart can. $15-$25.

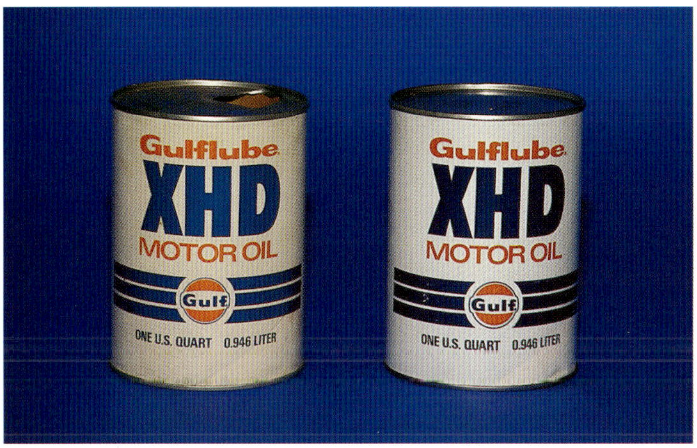

Gulfpride XHD, Left: 5/81 (CP) one-quart can; Right: 5/81 (CP) variation one-quart can. $15-$25.

Gulf Dextron II, Top: 4/80 (CP) one-quart can; Left: 4/80 (PC) one-quart can; Right: 11/84 (CP) one-quart can. $20-$30.

Gulf Super Duty, Left: 9/71 (PC) one-quart can; Right: 1/75 (PC) one-quart can. $15-$30.

Gulf Super Duty, Left: 8/80 (CP) one-quart can; Right: 8/80 (CP) one-quart can BP Oil. $15-$20.

Gulf ATF Type F, Left: 9/74 (CP) one-quart can; Right: 6/81 (CP) one-quart can. $20-$30.

Gulfpride Aviation, 1947 (SS) one-quart can. $50-$75.

Gulfpride Outboard, Left: 1/59 (SS) one-pint can; Right: 4/64 (SS) one-pint can. $20-$30 each.

Gulfpride Outboard, 8/62 (SS) 8-oz. can. $25-$35.

Gulfpride Marine H.D., 8/55 (SS) one-quart can. $150-$250. Rare.

Gulfpride Marine-G Outboard Motor Oil, 1977 (SS) 8-oz. can. $10-$15.

Gulfpride Marine Outboard, 5/51 (SS) one-quart can. $35-$65. Gulf Outboard Gear Oil with box, 4/51 (AL) 12-oz. $55-$75.

Gulf Antifreeze, 1/62 (SS) one-gallon can. Also sold in quart. $60-$80.

Gulf High Pressure Grease, 1920 (SS) one-pound can. $50-$75.

Gulf Antifreeze, Left: 4/68 (SS) one-quart can; Right: 4/64 (SS) one-quart can. $50-$75.

Gulf Supreme Cup Grease No. 3, 1938 (SS) one-pound can. $40-$60.

Gulf Antifreeze/Coolant, 2/69 (SS) one-quart can. $35-$45. This can had different graphics on both sides so the cans could be displayed seasonally.

Gulf Wheel Bearing Grease, 1940 (SS) one-pound can. $45-$65.

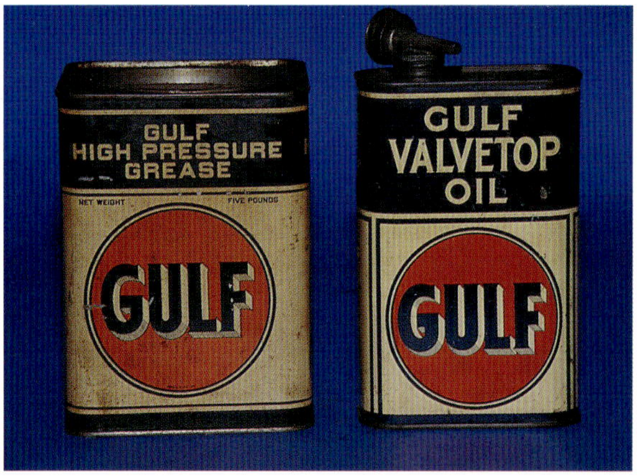

Gulf High Pressure Grease, five-pound can; Gulf Valve Top Oil, 1945 (SS) one-quart can. $50-$100.

Gulf Transmission Lubricant, 1940 (SS) 25-pound can. $75-$125.

Gulf Grease Cans, all 1948 (SS) one-pound cans. $35-$45 each.

Gulf Hypoid Gear Lubricant, 1938 (SS) 25-pound can. $75-$150.

Gulflex "A", Left 6/53 (SS) one-pound can; Right: 1/55 (SS) one-pound can. $20-$30 each.

Gulf Electric Motor Oil, 1943 (GB) 4-oz. $40-$60.

Gulfoil Household Lubricant, Left: 1940 (SS) 2-oz.; Right: 1940 (SS) 4-oz.
$50-$100 each.

Gulfoil, 2/57 (SS) 4-oz.; Lighter Fluid, 1948 (SS) 4-oz.; Electric Motor Oil,
8/50 (SS) 4-oz.; Penetrating Oil, 8/50 (SS) 4-oz. $30-$40 each.

Gulf Household Oil, 6/58 (SS) 4-oz.; Gulf Lighter Fluid, 6/58 (SS) 4-oz. $25-$35.

Gurley Refining Company
Memphis, TN

Thrift Motor Oil, 1966 (CP) one-quart can.
$15-$25.

Blue Diamond, 1965 (CP) one-quart can.
$25-$35.

John C. Hay Oil Company
Braintree, MA

Superior Motor Oil, 1958 (SS) one-quart can. $50-$75.

Hi Point Oils
Lorain, OH; Amarillo, TX; Sacramento, CA

Hi Point 2 Cycle, 1969 (CP) one-quart can. $25-$35.

Harley-Davidson
Milwaukee, WI

Harley-Davidson Pre-Luxe, 1961 (SS) one-quart can. $75-$125.

Hudson Oil Company
Kansas City, KS

Hudson Premium, 1960 (SS) one-quart can. $250-$375

Hudson Motor Oil, 1957 (SS) one-quart can. $250-$375

Hudson Pennveiw Motor Oil, 1954 (SS) one-quart can. $300-$500. Rare.

Hudson-Fisca Oil Company
Kansas City, KS

All 1968 (CP) one-quart cans. $20-$30 each.

Hudson Motor Oil, 1963 (SS) one-quart can. $30-$45.

Hudson Non Detergent, 1965 (CP) one-quart can; Hudson Hud Ultra Duty, 1965 (CP) one-quart can. $20-$40 each.

Hudson-Highway Oil Company
Working Man's Friend
Topeka, KS

Heavy Duty, 1968 (CP) one-quart can; Motor Oil, 1968 (CP) one-quart can. $15-$25.

Humble Oil & Refining Co; Standard Oil of New Jersey
Houston, TX

Polarine Transmission Oil, 1924 (SS) one-gallon can. $175-$275.

Standard Gear Compound, 1925 (SS) 5-pound can. $90-$150.

Esso Motor Oil (Uniflo), Left: 1935 (SS) one-quart can; Right: 1938 (SS) one-quart can. $35-$65 each.

Standard Penetrating Oil, 1925 (SS) one-quart can. $75-$125.

Essolube, 1934 (SS) one-quart can. $75-$125. Rare.

Esso Motor Oil (Uniflo), 1935-1938, side view.

Esso Uniflo, 1969 (SS) one-quart can. $25-$35; Essolube D-3, 1962 (CP) one-quart can. $50-$75. Rare.

Esso Motor Oil, Left: 1970 (SS) one-quart can; Right: 1968 one-quart can. $25-$35.

Esso Methanol Anti-freeze, Top: 1950 (SS) one-quart can; 1959 (SS) one-quart can, $35-$45 each; Esso Extra, 1965 (SS) one-quart can, $25-$35.

Essolube, Left: 1971 (SS) one-quart can; Right: 1970 one-quart can. $20-$30.

Esso Motor Oil, Top: (AL) (AL), Bottom: (SS) (SS) (AL) 1950s-1960,
all one-quart cans. $25-$35 each.

Essolube HDX, Left: 1971 (SS) one-quart can; Right: 1970 (CP) one-quart can. $20-$30.

Esso Tri-Rad Anti-freeze, 1939 (SS) one-quart can. $100-$175, Rare. Esso Turbo Oil, 1959 (SS) one-quart can. $50-$75.

Esso Outboard, Left: 1955 (SS) one-pint can; Right: 1950 (SS) one-pint can. $25-$35.

Esso Turbo Oil, Left: 1965 (SS) one-quart can; Right: 1965 (SS) one-quart can. $30-$45 each.

Aquaglide, Left: 1961 (SS) one-quart can; Right: 1963 (PB) one-quart can. $25-$35.

Esso Aquaglide Outboard, 1961 (SS) one-pint can. $15-$25.

Esso Fleet HD-20, 1960 (SS) five-gallon can. $25-$35.

Aquaglide, 1965 (PB) one-quart can. $10-$20.

Esso Handy Oil, 1938 (SS) 1-1/2 oz. $35-$65.

Esso Handy Oil, 1955 (SS) 4-oz. $25-$35; Esso Lighter Fluid, 4/38 (SS) 4-oz.; 1946 (SS) 4-oz. $30-$60.

Esso Handy Oil, Left to right: 1959 (SS) 4-oz.; 1963 (SS) 4-oz.; 1965 (SS) 4-oz. $15-$25.

Esso Lighter Fluid, Left: 1965 (SS) 4-oz.; Right: 1959 (SS) 4-oz. $15-$25.

Esso Hi-Temp, 1948 (SS) one-pound $25-$35; Esso Water Pump, 1954 (SS) one-pound $25-$35.

Esso Beacon Lubricant, 1940 (SS) one-pound $30-$45; Essoleum, Left: 1935 (SS) one-pound; Right: 1935 (SS) one-pound $40-$60.

Esso Grease, Top: 1963 (SS) one-pound; Left: 1961 (SS) one-pound; Right: 1961 (SS) one-pound $20-$30 each.

Enco Handy Oil, Left to right: 1959 (SS) 4-oz.; 1963 (SS) 4-oz.; 1965 (SS) 4-oz.; 1967 (SS) 4-oz. $15-$30.

Enco Grease, Top: 1963 (SS) one-pound; Left: 1961 (SS) one-pound; Right: 1961 (SS) one-pound $20-$30 each.

Encolube, 1966 (SS) one-quart can. $25-$45; Enco Motor Oil, 1968 (SS) one-quart can. $20-$40.

Enco Extra, 1966 (SS) one-quart can. $25-$35; Esso Snow Glide Snowmobile Oil, 1970 (SS) one-quart can. $25-$35.

Humble Outboard Motor Oil, 1956 (SS) one-quart can. $75-$125.

Humble Rust Ban 392, 1947 (SS) 4-oz. $50-$70; Humble Handy Oil, 1960 (SS) 4-oz.; 1963 (SS) 4-oz. $15-$30.

Oval E Water Pump, 1949 (SS) one-pound $40-$50.

Flashlike Lighter Fluid, 1943 (GB) 4-oz. $50-$100.

Pate Valve Glide, 1956 (SS) one-quart can. $55-$85.

Oval E Handy Oil, 1949 (SS) 4-oz. $50-$100.

Humble Cazar 3, 1955 (SS) one-pound $40-$60.

Humble Oil Division
Beacon Oil Company
Boston, MA

Beacon Grease, 1929 (SS) one-pound $225-$325.

Oilex Lubricating Oil, 1972 (CP) one-quart can. $15-$25.

Husky Oil Company
Cody, WY

Husky Heavy Duty, 1950s (SS) one-quart can. $350-$600.

Husky H/D Lube, 1966 (CP) one-quart can. Husky Hi-Power, 1966 (CP) one-quart can. $60-$80 each. Rare.

Husky Stratolube, 1970 (CP) one-quart can. $30-$50.

Husky S-3, 1970 (CP) one-quart can. $30-$40; Husky Outboard, 1966 (PB) one-quart can. $30-$40.

Hy Vis Oils
New York, NY

Hy Vis Motor Oil, Left: 1946 (SS) one-quart can; Right: 1956 (SS) one-quart can. $40-$60.

Hy Vis Oils, Left: 1964 (CP) one-quart can; Right: 1966 (CP) one-quart can. $20-$30 each.

Illinois Farm Supply
Bloomington, IL

Penn Bond, 1938 (SS) five-quart can. Also sold in quart. $50-$75.

Illinois Oil Products Inc.
Rock Island, IL

Welch Super Duty, 1965 (CP) one-quart can. $40-$60.

Independent Oil Company
Mansfield, OH

Jet Black Harness Oil, 1920 (SS) one-quart can. $75-$100; Our Jewel Axle Oil, 1928 (SS) one-quart can. $75-$100.

Industrial Lubricants Company
San Antonio, TX

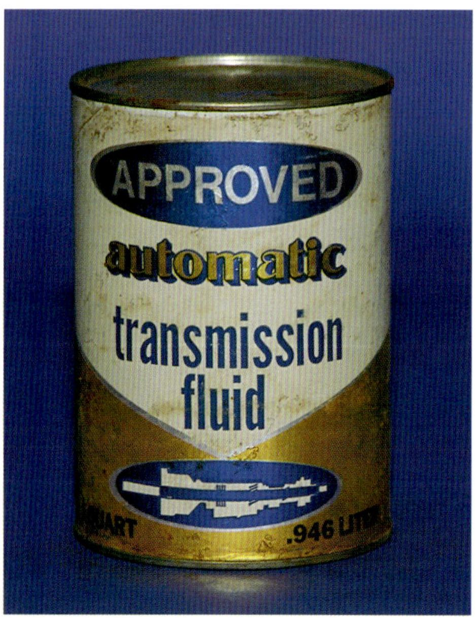

Approved ATF, 1977 (CP) one-quart can. $15-$25.

Intercontinental Lubricants Company
Brookfield, CT

Motor Guard, 1975 (CP) one-quart can. $15-$30.

International Harvester
Chicago, IL

McCormick-Deering Separator Oil, Copyright 1926, 1926 (SS) one-gallon can. $65-$95.

Interstate Oil Company
Kansas City, MO

Interstate X L, 1945 (SS) one-quart can. $75-$125.

Left: Type F, 1977 (CP); Right: Dextron II, 1977 (CP). $15-$25.

Interstate X L, 1959 (SS) one-quart can. $60-$75.

National Special, 1975 (CP) one-quart can. $15-$25.

Itasca Snowmobile Oil

Itasca Snowmobile Oil, 1970 (SS) one-quart can. $25-$35.

J & L Oil Company
Mundelein, IL

J & L Gas Non Detergent, 1970 (CP) one-quart can. $15-$25.

Jenney Manufacturing Company
Boston, MA

Jenney Solvenoil HD Premium, 1954 (SS) one-quart can. $75-$125.

Jenney Auto Oil, 1961 (SS) one-quart can. $50-$90.

Jewel Companies Inc.
Melrose Park, IL

Pace Setter Motor Oil, 1971 (CP) one-quart can. $15-$25.

John Deere
Moline, IL

Torq-Gard Supreme, 1971 (SS) one-quart can. Torq-Gard, 1965 (SS) one-quart can. $30-$60 each.

Chas. F. Kellom & Company
Philadelphia, PA

Invader Super All-Temp Motor Oil, 1961 (SS) one-quart can. $75-$125.

2000 Mile, 1948 (SS) one-quart can, $20-$30; Specialized, 1960 (SS) one-quart can, $15-$25; Dual Action, 1964 (SS) one-quart can. $15-$25.

Kendall Oil Corporation
Bradford, PA

Kendall 2000 Mile, 1943 (GB) one-quart jar. $35-$45.

Kendall Super B, Left: 1953 (SS) one-quart can; Right: 1959 (SS) one-quart can. $30-$40 each.

Kendall Motor Oil, Left: 1961 (AL) one-quart can; Right: 1963 (SS) one-quart can. $25-$35.

Kendall Gear Lube, 1940 (SS) one-pint can. $40-$60.

Keystone Lubricants
Philadelphia, PA

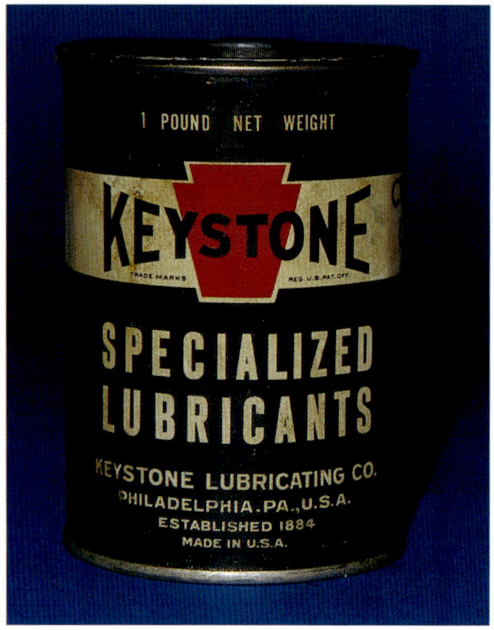

Keystone Specialized Lubricants, 1940 (SS) one-pound can. $25-$45.

Kentucky Consumers Oil Co. Inc.
Louisville, KY

Kay-Cee Motor Oil, 1946 (SS) one-quart can. $70-$90.

Kickhaefur Corporation
Beaver Dam, WI

Quicksilver Outboard, 1958 (SS) one-quart can. $40-$60.

PLACE
STAMP
HERE

SCHIFFER PUBLISHING LTD
4880 LOWER VALLEY ROAD
ATGLEN, PA 19310-9717 USA

WE HOPE THAT YOU ENJOY THIS BOOK...and that it will occupy a proud place in your library. We would like to keep you informed about other publications from Schiffer Books. Please return this card with your requests and comments.

Title of Book Purchased ____________________

❑ Purchased at: ____________________ ❑ received as a gift

Comments or ideas for books you would like to see us publish: ____________________

____

____

Your Name: ____________________

Address ____________________

City ____________________ State____ Zip________

E-mail Address ____________________

❑ Please send me a **free** *Schiffer Antiques, Collectibles, Arts and Design Catalog*

❑ Please send me a **free** *Schiffer Woodcarving, Woodworking, and Crafts Catalog*

❑ Please send me a **free** *Schiffer Military, Aviation, and Automotive History Catalog*

❑ Please send me a **free** *Whitford Body, Mind, and Spirit Catalog*

❑ Please send me information about new releases via email.
We don't share our mailing list with anyone

See our most current books on the web at **www.schifferbooks.com**

Contact us at: Phone: 610-593-1777; Fax: 610-593-2002; or E-mail: schifferbk@aol.com

SCHIFFER BOOKS ARE CURRENTLY AVAILABLE FROM YOUR BOOKSELLER

K: user\do\wp\basic\bouceback

Kitchen Oil Corporation
Stroud, OK

Super Shield Motor Oil, 1972 (CP) one-quart can. $15-$25.

KT Oil Corporation
El Dorado, KS

Elreco Motor Oil, 1954 (SS) one-quart can. $40-$60.

Vantage Motor Oil, 1979 (CP) one-quart can. $15-$25.

Le Hunt Oil and Gas Company
Cherryvale, KS

Logco Processed NRG Golden, 1945 (SS). $75-$100.

Marvlene ATF, 1961 (RS) one-quart can. $25-$35.

Leonard Refineries
Alma, MI

Leonard Duralube, 1965 (CP) one-quart can. $40-$60.

Lion Oil Company
El Dorado, AR

Lion Naturalube, 1950 (SS) one-quart can. $50-$75.

Lion Head Oil Company
Cleveland, OH

Lion's Head Premium, 1970 (CP) one-quart can. $25-$45.

Lou-Bob Co.

Lou-Bob Motor Oil Super Heavy Duty, 1959 (SS) one-quart can. $40-$60.

Lowe Oil Company
Clinton, MO

Champion Motor Oil, 1960 (SS) one-quart can. Champion ATF, 1965-1975 (CP) one-quart can. $20-$30 each.

Lubri-Loy Company
St. Louis, MO

Lubri-loy Oil Additive, 1958 (SS) one-quart can. $20-$40.

Gear-loy, Center: 1955 (SS) one-pint can; Lubri-Loy, Left: 1955 (SS) one-pint can; Lubri-Loy, Right: 1955 (SS) 4-oz. $10-$20.

Lubri-Gas International
Chicago, IL

Lubri-Gas Additive, 1960 (SS) one-quart can. $20-$40.

MacMillian Petroleum Company

**New York, NY; Chicago, IL;
Los Angeles, CA; El Dorado, AR**

MacMillan Ring-Free, Left: 1940 (SS) one-quart can; Right: 1946 (SS) one-quart can. $40-$60.

MacMillan Royal Scot, Left: 1963 (SS) one-quart can; Right: 1969 (CP) one-quart can. $25-$35.

MacMillan Ring-Free, Top: 10W30, 1963 (SS) one-quart can; Left: 20W50, 1973 (CP) one-quart can; Right: 4 Cycle, 1973 (CP) one-quart can. $20-$30 each.

Marathon Oil Company

Findlay, OH

Marathon Endurance, 1935 (SS) one-quart can. $275-$375.

Marathon Endurance, Top: 1973 (CP) one-quart can; Left: 1962 (SS) one-quart can; Right: 1965 (CP) one-quart can. $25-$35.

Marathon Permanent Anti-Freeze, 1958 (SS) one-gallon can. Also sold in one-quart can. $50-$75.

Marathon Antifreeze and Coolant, 1965 (SS) one-quart can. $40-$60.

Master Automotive Chemicals Inc.

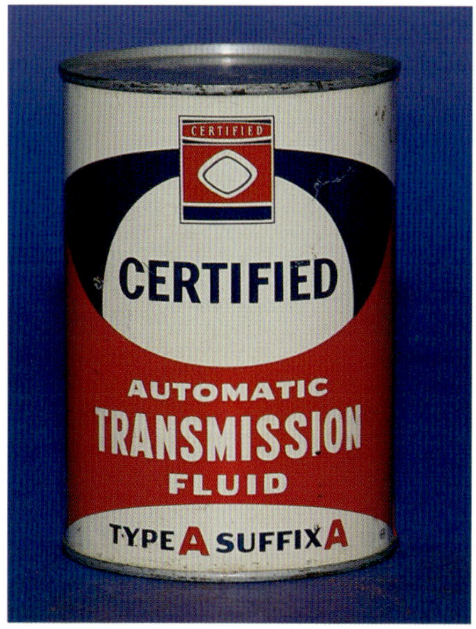

Certified ATF, 1959 (SS) one-quart can. $20-$30.

Maritime Oil Company
Houston, TX

Blue Pennant, 1934 (SS) one-quart can. $200-$300.

Maytag Inc.
Newton, IA

Maytag Household Oil, 1960 (SS) 8-oz. $45-$65.

Medallion Products Company
Chicago, IL

Gold Medallion ATF Type A, 1960 (SS) one-quart can. $25-$35.

Melcolene

Melcolene Series 1200 All Service (No company name or location) 1960 (SS) one-quart can. $25-$45.

Me-tee-or

Me-tee-or Motor Oil, 1960 (SS) one-quart can. $25-$35.

MFA. Oil Company

Columbia, MO; Memphis, TN

M.F.A. Axle Grease, 1929 (SS) three-pound can. $40-$60.

M.F.A. Mo-lube, Top: 1960 (SS) one-quart can; Left: Heavy Duty, 1970 (CP) one-quart can; Right: SHO-ME, 1969 (CP) one-quart can. $15-$35 each.

MFA DS-3 Diesel Motor Oil, 1963 (SS) one-quart can. $25-$35.

Mid States Dist. Co.
Mfg. for Harvest King
St. Paul, MN

Harvest King All Season, 1963 (RS) one-quart can; Harvest King Non Detergent, 1969 (CP) one-quart can. $20-$40.

Midwest Tire & Auto Sales
Milwaukee, WI

Mid-West All Weather, 1963 (SS) one-quart can. $25-$35.

Midstates Oil Company
Detroit, MI

Transol Washing Machine Transmission Oil, 1951 (SS) one-quart can. $50-$75.

Mintline & Company
Los Angeles, CA

Wigwam Eastern Motor Oil, 1960 (SS) 2-gallon can. $50-$75.

Mobil, Standard Oil of New York
White Eagle Division, Socony-Vacuum Oil Company
New York, NY

Socony Kerosene Oil, 1890-1900 (SS) one-gallon can. No estimate. This can would have been used to fill kerosene oil lamps in homes without electricity.

Socony Auto Spring Oil, 1925 (SS) one-quart can. $75-$125.

Gargoyle Mobil Oil A., 1925 (SS) one-quart can. $75-$95.

Socony Gear Oil, 1925 (SS) one-gallon can. $75-$125.

Socony Polarine, 1930 (SS) square 5-gal. can. $175-$250.

Mobiloil "C" for Gears, 1929 (SS) one-gallon can. $75-$125.

Mobiloil, AF, Arctic, Arctic Special, all 1935 (SS) one-quart cans. $75-$150.

Mobiloil, 1960 (SS) one-quart can; rare version, $50-$75; Mobiloil Special, 1962 (AL) one-quart can. $50-$75.

Lubrite Motor Oil, Left: 1934 (SS) one-quart can; Right: 1940 (SS) one-quart can. $50-$125 each.

Lubrite, 1953 (SS) two-gallon can. $35-$50.

Socony Lubrite, 1940 (SS) one-quart can, $55-$75; Magnolia Lubrite, 1940 (SS) one-quart can. $55-$75.

Lubrite, 1964 (CP) one-quart can; 1965 (CP) one-quart can. $20-$30.

Mobiloil Arctic, WW II vintage, 1943 (CP) one-quart can. $70-$90.

Mobil Cans, all 1966 (CP) one-quart can. $15-$30 each.

Mobil Permazone, 1963 (SS) one-quart can, $30-$40;
Mobil Freezone, 1963 (SS) one-quart can. $35-$45.

Mobil Fluid, Left: 1958 (SS) one-quart can; Right: 1959 (AL) one-quart can. $30-$50.

Mobil Permazone, Left: 1967 (SS) one-quart can;
Right: 1970 (SS) one-quart can. $25-$35 each.

Mobil Permazone, 1949 (SS) one-quart can. $35-$55.

Mobiloil Outboard, 1963 (PB) one-quart can. $15-$25.

Mobil Grease Outboard, 1956 (SS) two-pound can; Mobil Grease UW, 1945 (SS) two-pound can. $75-$125 each.

Socony Upperlub Oil, 1921 (SS) 4-oz. can, $90-$125; Socony Upperlube, 1929 (SS) 4-oz. can. $90-$125.

Mobil Handy Oil, 1964 (SS) 4-oz., $20-$30; Mobil Penetrating Oil, 1964 (SS) 4-oz. $20-$30.

Mobil Handy Oil, 1946 (SS) 4-oz. can, $25-$45; Mobil Penetrating Oil, 1948 (SS) 4-oz. can. $25-$45.

Mobil Grease, Left: 1941 (SS) one-pound; Middle: 1948 (SS) one-pound; Right: 1955 (SS) one-pound $30-$60 each.

Mobil Penetrating Oil, 1954 (SS) 4-oz., $25-$35; Mobil Handy Oil, 1956 (SS) 4-oz. $25-$35.

Mobil Grease No. 8, Power Chassis Lubricant, 1948 (SS) 8-oz. $40-$60.

Vilorette Oil, mfg. by Socony Vacuum Oil Co., 1940 (SS) 8-oz. $40-$60.

McCulloch Chain Saw Gear Case Oil, mfg. by General Petroleum Co., Mobilube SAE 140, 1954, $20-$40. Note dual flying horses.

White Eagle Cup Grease, 1934 (SS) five-pound can. $50-$75.

Wadhams Special Motor Oil, 1937 (SS) front. $125-$175.

White Eagle Grease, side view.

Wadhams Special Motor Oil, 1937 (SS) side view.

Monarch Petroleum Products
Columbus, OH

Monarch Petroleum Products Motor Oil, 1946 (SS) one-quart can. $50-$75.

Moores
Newark, OH

Moores All Season, 1955 (SS) one-quart can. $25-$35.

National Refining Company
En-Ar-Co
Cleveland, OH

Black Beauty Axle Grease, 1920 (SS) one-pound can. $50-$75.

R.E. Moore Company
Tyler, TX

Remco Motor Oil, 1947 (SS) one-quart can. $35-$55.

Mustang Dist. Co.
Troutdale, OR

Mustang Multi Viscosity, Mustang Heavy Duty, Mustang Non
Detergent, 6 variations of this can; 5 (CP) 1 (SS), 1975 all CP, one-quart cans.
$30-$60 each.

Black Beauty Axle Grease, 1925 (SS) one-pound can. $50-$75.

Niagara Lubricant Company
Buffalo, NY

Nia Penn Motor Oil, 1960 (SS) one-quart can. $40-$60.

Ohiolene Oil Company
Yonkers, NY

Ohiolene Motor Oil, 1960 (SS) one-quart can. $75-$100.

Oscar Bryant
Hollis, OK

Falcon Motor Oil, 1949 (SS) one-quart can. $35-$45.

Swift Motor Oil, 1949 (SS) one-quart can. $40-$60.

Nourse Oil Company
Kansas City, MO

Nourse Friction Proof Lubricant, 1970 (CP) one-quart can. $15-$25.

Oil Processing Corporation
Atlanta, GA

Dix Z Penn, 1970 (CP) one-quart can. $15-$25.

Outboard and Power Mower Oil

Outboard Motor and Power Mower Motor Oil, 1960 (SS) one-quart can. $75-$125.

Penaline Oils

Penaline Oils, 1948 (SS) one-quart can. $40-$60.

Pendurance

Pendurance, 1950 (SS) one-quart can. PA Oil Spec. #14. $125-$195.

Penn Central Oil Company
Kansas City, KS

Hi-Temp Dewaxed Motor Oil, 1940 (SS) one-quart can. $35-$45.

Penn Champ Oil Corporation
Butler, PA

Penn Champ 2000 Mile, 1939 (SS) one-quart can. No estimate.

Penn Champ Heavy Duty, 1961 (SS) one-quart can. $25-$35.

Penn Crest Oil & Grease Corp.
New York, NY

Bond Lube, 1954 (SS) one-quart can. $25-$35.

Pennsylvania Refining Co.
Butler, PA; Cleveland, OH; Edgewater, NJ

Thorobred Motor Oil, 1962 (SS) 2-gallon can. $45- $75.

Penn-Lloyd Oil Company

Polar Lube, 1938 (SS) one-quart can. $75-$125.

Pennzoil
Oil City, PA

Par-O-Vis Motor Oil, 1960 (SS) one-quart can; Pennzoil Motor Oil, 1950 (SS) one-quart can; Transport Motor Oil, 1956 (SS) one-quart can. $50-$75 each.

Petroleum Packers Inc.
Tampa, FL

Pennzoil Outboard, 1960 (SS) one-quart can. $30-$40.

Precision Motor Oil Aviation Type, 1965 (CP) one-quart can. $20-$30.

Penreco
Butler, PA

Penn Drake Outboard, 1963 (SS) one-quart can. $40-$60.

Penn Drake ATF, Penn Drake Motor Oil, Penn Drake HD Motor Oil, 1969 (SS) one-quart cans. $40-$60.

Phillips 66
Bartlesville, OK

Phillips 66 Aviation, 1959 (AL) one-quart can. $50-$75.

Phillips 66 Outboard, Left: 1955 (SS) one-pint can; Middle: 1960 (SS) one-pint can; Right: 1961 (SS) one-pint can. $15-$25 each.

Phillips 66, 1969 (CP) one-quart can. $15-$25 each.

Outboard Motor Oil, 1970 (CP) one-pint can, $10-$20; 2 Cycle Engine Oil, 1971 (CP) one-pint can. $10-$20.

Phillips 66 Handy Oil, 1958 (SS) 4-oz. $20-$30; Phillips 66 Lighter Fluid, 1959 (SS) 4-oz. $25-$35.

Phillips 66 Unique, 1960 (SS) two-gallon can. $30-$50.

Phillips 66 Grease, 1933 (SS) one-pound can. $50 – 475.

Pittsburgh Penn Oil Company
Pittsburgh, PA

Prize Penn Motor Oil, 1959 (SS) one-quart can. $25-$35.

Phillips 66 Grease, Left to right: 1956 (SS) one-pound; 1959 (SS) one-pound; 1966 (SS) one-pound; 1969 (SS) one-pound $25-$35 each.

Lub-O-Lene Motor Oil, 1968 (CP) one-quart can. $15-$25.

Premier Petroleum Company

Premier Motor Oil, 1963 (CP) one-quart can. $25-$35.

Protex Motor Oil

Protex Motor Oil, 1960 (SS) two-gallon can. $35-$45.

Pure Oil Company
Union Oil Company of California-
Pure Oil Division
Chicago, IL; Los Angeles, CA

Purelube Super Duty, 4/63 (SS) one-gallon can. $25-$35. Rare date variation.

Pure One-Fill Anti-Freeze, 1942/1948 one-quart can. $50-$75.

Pure Motor Oil/Purol, 1969 (CP) one-quart can. $30-$40 each.

One-Fill Anti-Freeze, Top: 56/4 (SS) one-gallon can; Left: 59/4 (SS) one-gallon can; Right: 59/4 (SS) one-gallon variation. $25-$35 each.

Purelube Outboard Motor Oil, 1954 (54-1) (SS) one-quart can. $40-$60.

Purelube Outboard (Side view)

Pure Outboard, 1953 (GB) one-quart glass bottle. $50-$75.

Purol Household Oil, 1936 (SS) 4-oz., $125-$225; Pure Household Oil, Left: 1940 (SS) 4-oz.; 1943 (GB) 4-oz. $45-$75 each.

Pure Sure Household Oil, 53-4 (SS) 4-oz.; Pure Sure Lighter Fluid, 1953 (SS) 4-oz. $40-$60 each.

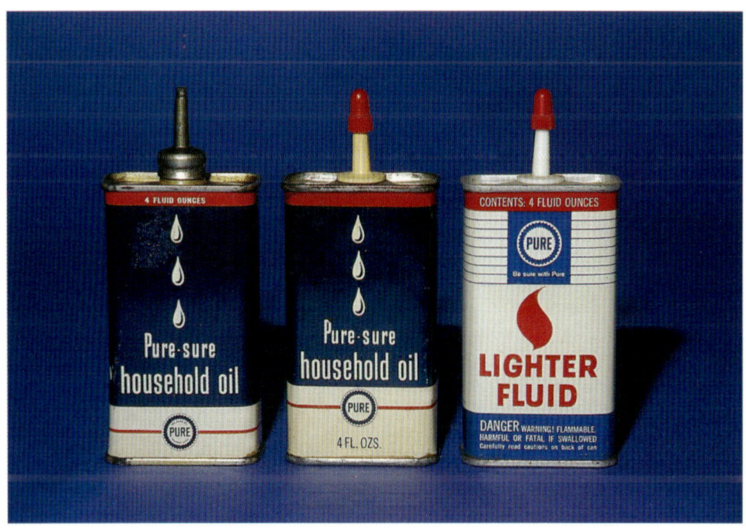

Pure Sure Household Oil, Left: 1955 (SS) 4-oz.; Right: 1969 (SS) 4-oz.; Pure Lighter Fluid, 4/62 (SS) 4-oz. $30-$60.

Tiolene Wheel Bearing, 1941 (SS) one-pound can. $40-$70.

Purelube Chassis W, 1956 (SS) 5-pound can, $35-$45; Tiolene Grease, 1935 (SS) one-pound can. $40-$70.

Pure Sure RU Glide, 4/57 (SS) one-gallon can. $30-$40.

Pure RU Glide, 62/4 (SS) one-gallon can. $35-$45.

Pure High HP Purelube Pump Topper, 1954. $200-$400. These were affixed to the top of the gas pump upon the introduction of a new product. Typically they would spin with the wind and would have discarded after a period of time.

Pyroil Inc.
Lacrosse, WI

Pyroil All Season, 1961 (SS) one-quart can. $25-$45.

Quaker Oil Corporation
St. Louis, MO

Quaker Maid Super 10W30, 1966 (CP) one-quart can. $15-$25.

Quaker Maid Supreme 10W40, 1975 (CP) one-quart can. $10-$25.

Quaker State Oil and Refining Company
Oil City, PA

Quaker State Medium Heavy Oil, 1920 (SS) one-gallon can. $75-$125.

Penn Seal Motor Oil, 1934 (SS) one-quart can. $45-$65.

Penn Seal Motor Oil, 1938 (SS) one-quart can. $40-$60.

Deluxe Motor Oil, 1965 (SS) one-quart can. $25-$35.

Duplex Outboard Special, Left: 1955 (SS) one-quart can; Right: 1950 (SS) one-quart can, $50-$125 each; Duplex Marine Engine Oil, 1955 (SS) one-gallon can. $75-$150.

Sterling Lubricant, 1940 (SS) one-pound can. $40-$60.

Quaker Supreme Chemical Company

Montgomery, AL

Motor Supreme Motor Oil, 1970 (CP) one-quart can. $15-$20 each.

Mendel Motor Oil, 1971 (CP) one-quart can. $15-$20.

Quality Oil Company
Topeka, KS

PermaFilm, 1962 (RS) one-quart can. $25-$35.

Red Head Oil Company
Wooster, OH

Redoco Premium Quality, 1963 (SS) one-quart can. $40-$60.

Riley Bros. Inc.
Burlington, IA

Riley Bros. Motor Oil, 1950 (SS) one-quart can. $40-$60.

R-B 500, 1960 (SS) one-quart can. $20-$30.

Red Giant Oil Company
Council Bluff, IA

Red Giant, 1967 (CP) one-quart can. $25-$35.

Riley Bros. Washing Machine Oil, 1950 (SS) one-quart can. $40-$60.

Riley Bros. Cream Separator Oil, 1950 (SS) one-quart can. $40-$60.

Royal Oil Company
Baltimore, MD

Jet Motor Oil, 1955 (SS) one-quart can. $30-$40.

Rocket Distributors
Seattle, WA

Rocket Anti-Freeze, 1960 (SS) one-gallon can. $45-$65.

Royal Crown

Royal Crown 100% Pennsylvania, 1935 (SS) two-gallon can. $40-$60.

Royal Triton Company
Des Plaines, IL

Royal Triton Multi-Grade, 1973 (CP) one-quart can; Royal Triton HD, 1973 (CP) one-quart can. $20-$30. This company bought the rights to Royal Triton from Union Oil Company.

Royal Windsor Petroleum Company
Philadelphia, PA

Royal Windsor Motor Oil, 1957 (SS) one-quart can. $40-$65.

Searle Petroleum Company
Omaha, NE

Extreme Range Motor Oil, 1949 (SS) one-quart can. $40-$60

Seaboard Oil Company
Doraville, GA

Seaboard Motor Oil, 1960 (SS) one-quart can. $225-$425.

Sears, Roebuck & Company
Chicago, IL

Cross Country Anti-Freeze, 1935 (SS) one-gallon can. $40-$70.

Champion Graphite Axle, 1930 (SS) one-pound can. $30-$50.

Security Oil Company
Wichita, KS

Wings, Left: Grease, 1950 (SS) 10-pound can; Right: Anti-Freeze, 1954 (SS) one-gallon can. $50-$75 each.

Shaffer Oil and Refining Company
Chicago, IL

Deep Rock Motor Oil, 1930 (SS) one-gallon can. $125-$225.

Service Plus Distributing Company
Albemarle, NC

Service Regular Motor Oil, 1960 (SS) two-gallon can. $40-$60.

Service Plus Motor Oil, 1970 (SS) one-quart can. $35-$45.

Shamrock Oil and Gas Company
Amarillo, TX

LP NG, 1970 (CP) one-quart can. $30-$40.

Shelby Petroleum Company
LaFollette, TN

Sail Motor Oil, 1971 (CP) one-quart can. $20-$30.

Peer Heavy Duty Motor Oil, 1975 (CP) one-quart can. $15-$20.

Shell Rotella/Rimula, 1960s-1970s (CP) one-quart cans. $25-$35.

Shell Oil Company
Houston, TX

Golden Shell, 1957 (RS) one-quart can. $35-$45.

Shell Engine Conditioning Oil, 1962 (SS) one-quart can. $25-$45.

Shell Outboard, 1952 (SS) five half pints. $25-$45.

Super Shell, Left: 1966 (SS) one-quart; Right: 1969 (SS) one-quart. $35-$65. Rare.

Shell Outboard, Left: 1956 (SS) one-pint can; Middle: 1961 (SS) 6-oz.; Right: 1963 (SS) one-pint can. $25-$35.

Shell Handy Oil, 1947 (SS) 4-oz. $65-$125.

Shell Anti-Freeze Alcohol Type, 1960 (SS) one-quart can. $40-$60. Rare.

Shell Outboard, Left: 1965 (SS) one-pint can; Right: 1969 (SS) one-pint can. $15-$25 each.

Shell Handy Oil, Soap Box Derby Lubricant, Left to right: 1957 (SS) 4-oz. can; 1957 (SS) 4-oz. can; 1963 (SS) 4-oz. can. $25-$150.

Shell Lighter Fluid, 1940 (SS) 4-oz. $75-$150.

Shell Lighter Fluid, Left to right: 1955 (SS); 1964 (SS); 1962 (SS) 4-oz. cans. $35-$45.

Shell Grease, Left: 1940 (SS); Right: 1948 (SS) one-pound cans. $35-$45.

Shell Grease Retinax, Top: 1954 (SS) one-pound can; Right: 1951 (SS) one-pound can; Left: 1954 (SS) one-pound can.
$25-$35 each.

Super Shell Gasoline. Shell underseat gas can. Variation from Wayco Oil Co., a large Shell distributor in Detroit, MI.

Shell Grease, Top: 1963 (SS) one-pound can; Left: 1956 (SS) one-pound can; Right: 1958 (SS) one-pound can. $20-$30 .

Shell Products, 1947 (SS) five-gallon can. $25-$45.

Aero Shell Grease, 1956 (SS) one-pound can.
$50-$75.

Aeroshell Fluid, 1956 (SS) one-gallon can, $25-$35; Shell Retinax A Grease, 1956 10-pound can.
$25-$35.

Shell Underseat Gasoline Can, 1915 (SS) one-gallon can. $250-$450. Rare and dual collectible.

Shell Donax P Penetrating Oil, 1956 (SS) one-gallon can, $25-$35; Shell Donax R Rubberlube, 1956 (SS) one-gallon can. $30-$40.

Shell X100 Premium Pump Topper, 1957. $200-$400.

Signal Oil Company
Los Angeles, CA

Signal Motor Oil Premium, 1956 (SS) one-quart can. $50-$100.

Sinclair Oil and Refining Company
Pierce Petroleum Company
(Pierce Petroleum was bought by Sinclair in the 1920s)
New York, NY

Pennant Hy-Glo Oil, 1925 (SS) one-quart can. $125-$225.

Pierce Pennant Oil, Left: 1927 (SS) 1/2-gallon can.; Right: 1930 (SS) 1/2-gallon can. $200-$400 each.

Sinclair Dino Oil, Left to right: 1965 (CP) one-quart can. $35-$45 each.

Sinclair Opaline Motor Oil, 1920s (SS) 1/2-gallon can. $375-$475.

Sinclair Dino Supreme, Extra Duty, Dinolene, Econoil, Left to right: 1969 (CP) one-quart cans. $20-$30 each.

Dino Supreme, 1964 (CP) one-quart can; Dinolene (variation) 1964 (CP) one-quart can. $30-$40 each.

Sinclair Opaline, 1934 (SS) one-quart can. Copper top version. $50-$100.

Sinclair Tenol Motor Oil, 1954 (SS) one-quart can. $40-$60.

Tenol Motor Oils—Red Top: Left: 1969 (CP) one-quart can; Yellow Top: Right: 1969 (CP) one-quart can, $25-$35. Sold in top colors, blue, red, black, green, white and yellow to indicate grade.

Sinclair Turbo-S, 1961 (SS) one-quart can. $35-$50.

Sinclair Outboard, 1963 (SS) one-pint can. $20-$30.

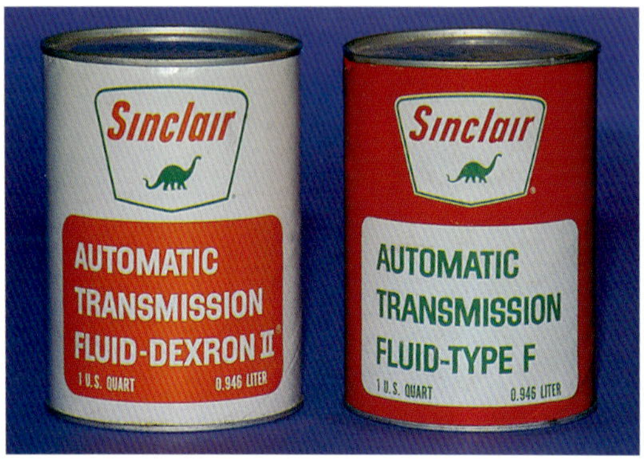

Sinclair ATF-Dextron II, Sinclair ATF-Type F 1969 (CP) one-quart can. $20-$30 each.

Sinclair Household Oil, 1940 (SS) 4-oz., $40-$60; Sinclair Lighter Fluid, 1953 (SS) 4-oz. $50-$75.

Sinclair Outboard Motor Oil, 1954 (SS) one-quart can. $50-$75.

Sinclair Methanol Anti-Freeze, Left: 1949 (SS) one-quart can; Right: 1959 (SS) one-quart can. $45-$75 each.

Sinclair Super Anti-Freeze, 1947 (SS) one-gallon can. $35-$45. Not known in one-quart size.

Household Oil/Lighter Fluid, Left to right: 1953 (SS) 4-oz.; 1953 (SS) 4-oz.; 1963 (SS) 4-oz.; 1965 (SS) 4-oz. $25-$35 each.

Sinclair Cup Grease, 1929 (SS) one-pound can. $75-$125.

Sinclair No. 3 Cup, 1934 (SS) one-pound can, $50-$75; Sinclair Litholine, Left: 1957 (SS) one-pound can; Right: 1959 (SS) one-pound can. $35-$45.

Sinclair Wax Oil, 1926 (SS) one-quart can. $50-$75.

Sioux Oil Company
New Castle, WY

Sioux Motor Oil, 1960 (SS) one-quart can. $75-$150.

Skelly Oil Company
Tulsa, OK

Tagoline Lubricants, 1940 (SS) one-pound can. $40-$60.

Skelly Supreme, 1963 (SS) one-pound can. $25-$35.

Southern Oil Company of New York, Inc.

Rotary Motor Oil (SOCO), 1949 (SS) 2-gallon can. $40-$60.

Southport Oil Company
Texas City, TX; Kilgore, OK; New Orleans, LA

Hiofilm Dynamic Lubrication, 1935 (SS) one-quart can. No estimate of value. Rare.

Southport Super Oil, Left: 1935 (SS) one-quart can; Right: 1937 (SS) one-quart can. No estimate of value. Rare.

Sovereign Oil Company
Chicago, IL

Monarch Super Motor Oil, 1966 (CP) one-quart can. $15-$30.

Community Motor Oil, 1971 (CP) one-quart can. $15-$25. Packaged by Soverign Oil Co., Chicago IL for Community Discount Stores.

Specialty Oil Company
Shreveport, LA; Little Rock, AR; Jackson, MS

Gold Band Motor Oil, 1970 (CP) one-quart can. $15-$25.

Standard Oil Company of Kentucky
Louisville, KY

Standard Oil Household Oil, 1930 (SS) 4-oz. $225-$425.

Standard Oil Motor Cup Grease, 1959 (SS) one-pound $45-$75.

Standard Oil Product Can, 1960 (SS) five-gallon can. $40-$60.

Standard Oil five-gallon product can, 1963 (SS). $30-$50.

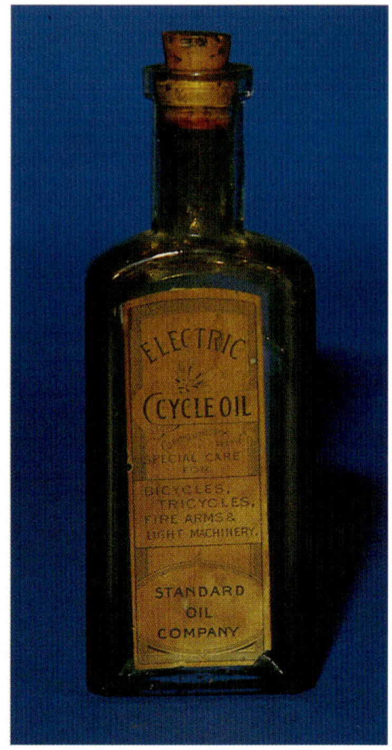

Electric Cycle Oil, 1890 (Glass) 4-oz. $700-$1000.

Standard Oil; Sohio; BP; Fleet-Wing
Cleveland, OH

Standard Oil Grease Bucket, 1890 (Wood) 10-lbs. No estimate.

Standard Oil Household Lubricant, Left: 1905 (SS) 4-oz.; Right: 1909 (SS) 8-oz. $175-$375.

Electric Cycle Oil, 1905 (SS) 8-oz. $325-$425.

Electric Cycle Oil (Side view)

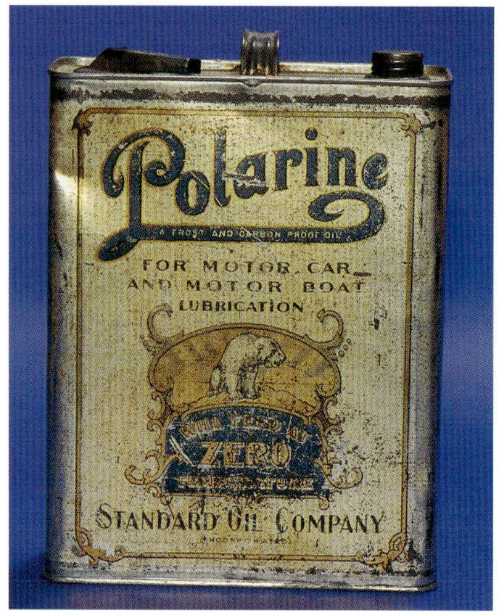

Polarine Motor Oil, 1910 (SS) one-gallon can. $125-$250.

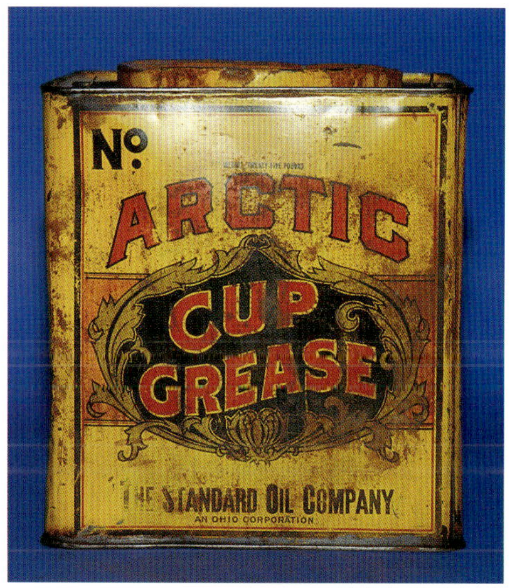

Standard Oil Arctic Cup Grease, 1916 (SS) 25-lbs. $175-$275.

Standard Oil Co. Ohio Household Lubricant, 1910 (SS) 4-oz., $125-$200; Standard Oil Co. California, Household Lubricant, 1910 (SS) 4-oz. $125-$200.

Standard Oil of Ohio Arctic Cup Grease, 1920 (SS) 25-lbs. $75-$150.

Ruddy Harvester Oil, 1900 (SS) five-gallon can. $275-$375.

Standard Gas Engine Oil, 1910 (SS) five-gallon can. $50-$75.

Standard Oil of Ohio Herdoil, 1925 (SS) one-gallon can. $85-$135.

Ruddy Harvester Oil, 1910 (SS) one-quart can. $95-$175.

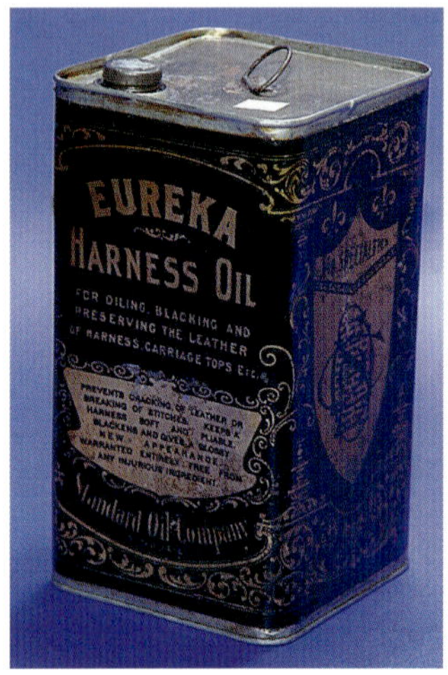

Eureka Harness Oil, 1910 (SS) one-gallon can. $75-$150.

Thresher Hard Oil, 1908 (SS) 25-pound can. $175-$275.

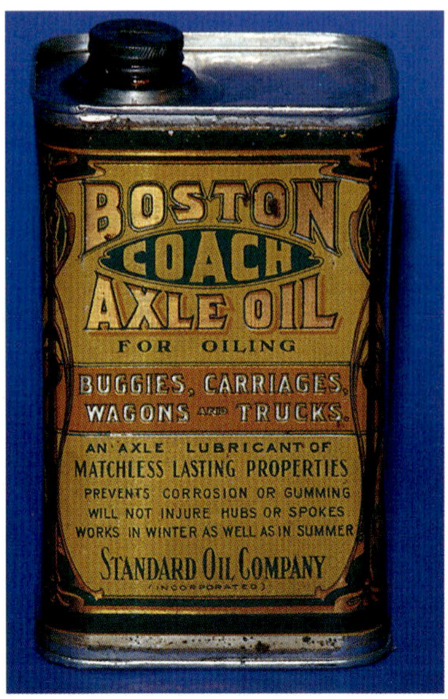

Boston Coach Axle Oil, 1910 (SS) one-quart can. $75-$150.

NeatsFoot Oil, 1910 (SS) one-quart can; Hoof Oil, 1910 (SS) one-quart can. $75-$125 each.

Polarine Spring Lubricant, 1925 (SS) 12-oz. No estimate.

Polarine Cup Grease, Left: 1927 (SS) one-pound; Right: 1928 (SS) one-pound $50-$75 each.

Polarine Pressure Gun Grease, 1927 (SS) one pound $40 $60.

Standard Anti-Freeze, 1926 (SS) five-gallon can. $125-$175.

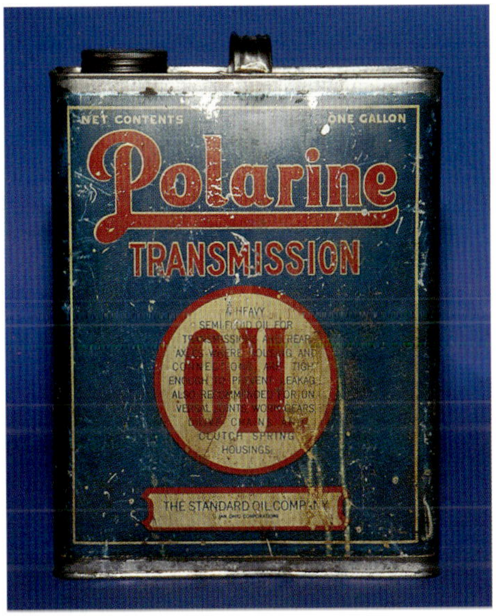

Polarine Transmission Oil, 1927 (SS) one-gallon can. $125-$225.

Sohio Leather Dressing, 1928 (SS) one-pint can. $60-$80.

Household Lubricating Oil, 1918 (SS) 4-oz. $125-$225.

Sohio Plumbers Cutting Oil, 1935 (SS) one-gallon can. $75-$125.

Sohio Motor Oil, 1934 (SS) five-quart can. $75-$125. Rare

Sohio HQ, 1943 (GB) one-quart glass jar. No estimate.

Sohio Nitron, 5/66-1975, one-quart can, $15-$25; Sohio Nitron, 1975, one-quart can, $10-$20.

Renown, Left: 1933 (SS) two-gallon can; Right: 1938 (SS) two-gallon can. $75-$225 each.

Sohio Facto, 1966-1969, one-quart can; Sohio Facto, 1969-1975, one-quart can. $15-$25 each.

Sohio Multron, 5/66-1965, one-quart can, $15-$25; Sohio Multron, 1975, one-quart can, $10-$20.

Sohio Facto, 1975, one-quart can; Sohio Facto Supreme, 1975, one-quart can. $10-$20 each.

Sohio Mica Axle Grease, 1928-1946, one-pound can. $25-$35.

Sohio Lubtec, 10/56-62, one-poundcan; Sohio Grease Cans, 1959-1962, one-pound can. $20-$30 each.

Sohio Grease Cans, 1935-1946, one-pound cans. $25-$35 each.

Sohitran #2, 1966, one-pound can; Sohio Lubtec, Sohio Lubtec L, 1962-2/64, one-pound cans. $25 $35 each.

Sohio Grease, 1944, one-lb can; Sohio Cup Grease, Sohio Chassis Lubricant, 1955, one-pound can. $25-$35 each.

Top: Golden Duron, 1965 (SS) one-gallon can; Right: Premex, 1964 (SS) one-gallon can; Left: HQD, 1964 (SS) one-gallon can. $30-$40 each.

Sohio Home Oil, 1958 (SS) 4-oz.; Sohio Lighter Fluid, 1954 (SS) 4-oz.; Sohio Penetrating Oil, 1955 (SS) 4-oz. $35-$45 each.

Sohio Boat Care Kit, 1957 (PB) (GB) (SS). $300-$600.

Sohio Home Oil, 1962 (SS) 4-oz.; Sohio Lighter Fluid, 1962 (SS) 4-oz. $25-$35 each.

Sohio Car Care Kit, 1953 (GB) (SS). $250-$350.

Sohio Outboard Gear Oil, Left: 1956 (SS) one-quart can; Right: 1960 (PB) one-quart can. $50-$100 each. Both rare.

Fleet-Wing Medium Graphite, 1934 (SS) one-pound can. $40-$65.

Fleet-Wing Motor Oil, 1934 (SS) one-quart can. $75-$175.

Fleet-Wing Piston Seal, 1970 (SS) one-quart can. $20-$30.

Fleet-Wing Penn Motor Oil, 1940 (SS) one-quart can. $125-$225.

Fleet-Wing 7 C's Outboard, 1957 (SS) one-quart can. $50-$75. Rare.

Fleet-Wing MG, 1970 (SS) one-quart can; Fleetwing HD, 1970 (SS) one-quart can. $25-$35 each.

Boron All Season, 1975 (CP) one-quart can. Top variations. $10-$20.

Super Visco-Static Motor Oil, 1970 (CP) one-quart can. $15-$25.

BP Auto Oil, 1970 (CP) one-quart can. $10-$20.

Stewart-Warner
Alemite Division
Chicago, IL

Super Long Life, 1976 (CP) one-quart can; Super Heavy Duty, 1976 (CP) one-quart can. $15-$25 each.

STP Corporation
Miami, FL

STP Motor Oil, STP Motor Oil 10W40, Left: 1974 (CP) one-quart can; Right: 1977 (CP) one-quart can. $15-$30 each.

Sterno Corporation
New York, NY

Sterno Carbon Remover, 1929 (SS) one-quart can; $50-$75. Not oil but a very early graphic auto product can.

STP Motor Oil, 1976 (CP) one-quart can. $15-$25.

J. B. Street & Company
Maryland Heights, MO

Zephyr Motor Oil, 1980 (CP) one-quart can. This is a can bank. $15-$25.

H. D. Summers Company
Kansas City, MO

Sumco All Weather, 1961 (SS) one-quart can. $25-$35.

Studebaker Auto Sales Co.
Parts Division
South Bend, IN

S-P Special Motor Oil, 1959 (SS) one-quart can. $45-$65.

Sunoco
Philadelphia, PA

Sunoco Motor Oil, 1920 (SS) one-gallon can. $275-$375.

Sunoco Outboard, 1960 (SS) one-pint can. $15-$25.

Sunoco Anti-freeze, 1959 (SS) one-gallon can. Also sold in one-quart. $25-$45.

Sunoco Household Oil, Left: 1935 (SS) 4-oz.; Right: 1937 (SS) 4-oz. $25-$65 each.

Sunoco Lighter Fluid, Left: 1960 (SS) 4-oz.; Right: 1965 (SS) 4-oz. $30-$50 each.

Sunoco Household Oil, 1956 (SS) 4-oz.; 1963 (SS) 4-oz.; 1969 (SS) 4-oz. $25-$35 each.

Sunoco Lighter Fluid, 1960, 1965 Reverse side.

Sunoco Household Oil, 1956, 1963, 1969 Reverse side.

Sunoco Water Pump Grease, Left: 1934 (SS) one-pound can; Right: 1937 (SS) one-pound can. $25-$55 each.

Sunoco Motor Cup, Left: 1937 (SS) one-pound can; Right: 1947 (SS) one-pound can. $25-$35 each.

Sunoco Prestige Grease, 1960 (CP) one-pound can, $20-$30; Sunoco HD, Left: 1958 (CP) one pound can, Right: 1958 (CP) one-pound can, $25-$35.

Techna Crude Oil Sales Company of America

Heavy Duty Reclaimed Motor Oil, 1958 (SS) one-quart can. $375-$475.

Superior Products
North Portland, OR

Standby Regular, 1969 (CP) one-quart can, $20-$30; Standby Outboard, 1969 (CP) one-quart can, $25-$35.

Tenneco Oil Co.
Houston, TX

All 1980 (CP) one-quart cans. $15-$25 each.

Tennessee Farmers Coop
Lavergne, TN

Director, +200, Gold Film, all 1969 (CP) one-quart can. $20-$30.

Texaco
New York, NY

Texaco Spica Oil, 1915 (SS) one-pint can, $225-$325; Texaco 574 Oil, 1930 (SS) one-quart can, $90-$130.

New Texaco Airplane Oil, 1940s (SS) one-quart can, $1500-$2500. Only a few known to exist.

Texaco Outboard, 1950 (GB) one-pint. $50-$75.

Texaco PT Anti-Freeze, 1945 (SS) one-quart can. $50-$75. Rare.

Texaco Motor Oil, 11/68 (CP) one-quart can, $20-$30. Rare composite variation.

Havoline Pressure Gun, 1931 (SS) one-pound can. $40-$60.

Texaco Household Oil, Left to right: 1946 (SS) 3-oz.; 1953 (SS) 4-oz.; 1962 (SS) 4-oz.; 7/60 (SS) 4-oz. $30-$60 each.

Texaco Grease, Left: 9/66 (SS) ten-pound can; Right: 1920 (SS) one-pound can. $30-$75 each.

Texstar Inc.
St. Louis, MO

Duplex Non Detergent, 1980 (CP) one-quart can. $15-$25.

Duplex ATF, 1980 (CP) one-quart can. $15-$20.

Thompson Products
Cleveland, OH

Thompson Products Aerotype Break-in Motor Oil made expressly for Thompson Products by Standard Oil of California (Chevron), 1945 (SS) one-quart can. $75-$150.

Thonis Oil Magic; Benzol Gas Stations
Miami, FL

Thonis Motor Oil, Left: 1975 (CP) one-quart can; Right: 1975 (CP) one-quart can. $15-$25 each.

Tidewater Oil Service
Mathews, VA

Tidewater Motor Oil, 1959 (SS) one-quart can. $20-$30.

Thriftlube Oil Company
Philadelphia, PA

Thriftlube Motor Oil, 1950 (SS) one-quart can. $40-$60.

Topsall Lubricants
Cleveland, OH

Topsall Super Motor Oil, 1960 (SS) one-quart can. $25-$35. *Courtesy Mr. Pat Quail.*

Tradco Corporation
Akron, OH

Tradco Quality, 1978 (SS) one-quart can; Tradco ATF, 1978 (SS) one-quart can. $25-$35 each.

Trek High Test Anti Freeze

Trek High Test Anti-Freeze, 1940 (SS) one-quart can. $35-$45.

Troco Oil Company,
Tulsa, OK

Troco Motor Oil, Top: 1969 (CP) one-quart can; Left: 1960 (SS) one-quart can; Right: 1965 (CP) one-quart can. $20-$30 each.

Tresler Oil Company
Cincinnati, OH

Tresler Comet Premium H.D., 1955 (SS) one-quart can. $65-$85.

Ultra Penn Refining Company
Butler, PA

Ultra Penn Motor Oil, 1937 (SS) one-quart can. $80-$125.

Unilube Products
W. Memphis, AR

Unilube Quality Motor Oil, 1972 (CP) one-quart can. $15-$25.

Union Carbide
Consumer Products Division

Prestone Motor Oil, 1958 (SS) one-quart can. $35-$55.

Prestone Anti-freeze, Left: 1947 (SS) one-quart can; Middle: 1958 (SS) one-quart can; Right: 1963 (SS) one-quart can. $30-$60 each.

Prestone Anti-freeze, Left: 1965 (SS); Right: 1969 (CP) one-quart cans. $25-$35 each.

Union Oil Company of California
Los Angeles, CA

Triton TBX Engine Break-in Oil, 1955 (SS) one-quart can, $75-$150, rare; 76 Union Triton, 1947 (SS) one-quart can, $35-$55.

76 Union Royal Triton, 1966 (CP) one-quart can. $25-$35.

76 Union Long Distance Purple, 1977 (CP) one-quart can. $15-$25. One of the more colorful composite cans produced.

Red Line Lubricants, 1947 (SS) one-pound can. $40-$60.

76 Union Triton Premium, 1946 (SS) one-quart can; 76 Union Grease, 1966 (SS) ten-pound can. $30-$60 each.

United Co-operatives, Inc.
Alliance, OH

Bureau-Penn Motor Oil, 1940 (SS) two-gallon can. $40-$60.

Bureau-Penn two-gallon can. Reverse side.

Unico Outboard Motor Oil, 1956 (SS) one-quart can. $25-$55.

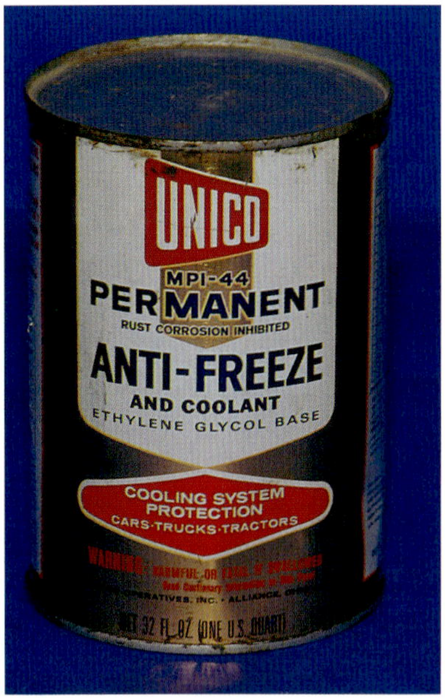

Unico Anti-Freeze and Coolant, 1969 (SS) one-quart can. $25-$35.

United Laboratories
Dumas, AR

UNI Motor Oil, 1976 (CP) one-quart can. $15-$20.

United Oil and Grease
Abilene, TX

Zeroil Motor Oil, 1953 (SS) one-quart can. $40-$60.

United Oil Manufacturing Company

United Paraffine Base, 1961 (SS) one-quart can. $25-$35.

Universal Motor Oil Company
Wichita, KS

Universal Motor Oil, 1969 (CP) one-quart can. $15-$25.

Universal Anti-Freeze, 1960 (SS) one-quart can. $20-$30.

Wadsworth Oil Company
Chickasa, OK

Oil King, 1973 (CP) one-quart can. $15-$25.

Wake Up Viz

Wake Up Viz, 1958 (SS) 2-gallon can. $65-$95.

Warden Oil Company
Minneapolis, MN

Vim Non Detergent, 1959 (SS) one-quart can. $25-$35.

Warren Oil Company
Dunn, NC

Warren Motor Oil, 1970 (CP) one-quart can. $15-$25.

Warren Refining Company
Cleveland, OH

BusTrux Motor Oil, 1950 (SS) one-quart can. $20-$40.

Warwick Labs
Rahway, NJ

Fox Head 10W30, 1970 (CP) one-quart can. $20-$30.

Fox Head Motor Oil, 1970 (CP) one-quart can. $20-$30.

Fox Head XLM, 1975 (CP) one-quart can; Fox Head Diesel Turbo, 1975 (CP) one-quart can. $10-$20 each

Westland Oil Company
Minot, ND

Dura Non Detergent, 1959 (SS) one-quart can. $25-$35.

Dura Motor Oil, 1951 (SS) one-quart can. $50-$75.

White and Bagley Company
Makers of Oilzum
Distributed by SAAB Motors Company
Hingham, MA

SAAB Two Cycle Engine Oil, 1965 (SS) one-quart can. $35-$55.

White Motor Corporation
Oakbrook, IL; Cleveland, OH

Farm Engine Super, 1969 (CP) one-quart can. $15-$25.

White Permanent Anti-Freeze, 1957 (SS) one-quart can. $40-$60.

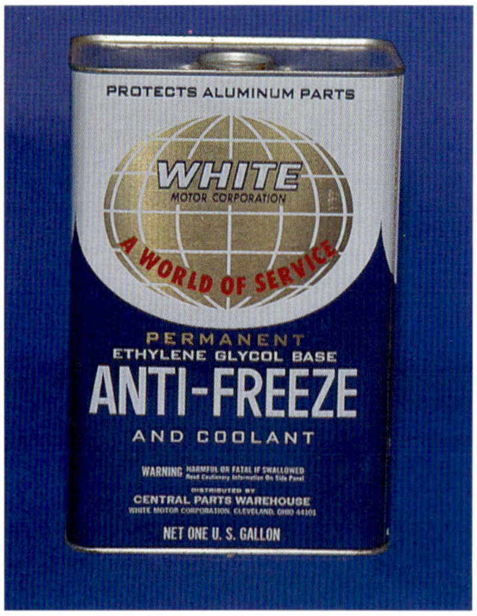

White Anti-Freeze, 1965 (SS) one-gallon can. $25-$35.

Hydraulic Oil, Supreme Blend Motor Oil, 1971 (CP) one-quart cans. $15-$25 each.

Harold R. Wilkinson
Spencer, NY; W. Haverstraw, NY

Modernized Multi-Lube, 1947 (SS) one-quart can. $30-$40.

Windsor-Lloyd Products Inc.
Philadelphia, PA

De Kent ATF, 1978 (CP) one-quart can.
$15-$25.

Wolf Head
Oil City, PA; New York, NY

Empire Motor Oil, 1945 (SS) one-quart can. $55-$85.

Wolf Head Outboard, 1960 (SS) one-quart can. $20-$30.

Wolf Head Motor Oil, Left: 1958 (SS) one-quart can; Right: 1961 (SS) one-quart can. $20-$30 each.

Work Force
Houston, TX

Work Force Motor Oil, 1973 (CP) one-quart can. $10-$20.

Wyeth Hardware & Manufacturing Company
St. Joseph, MO

Shield Separator Oil, 1950 (SS) one-quart can. $40-$60

Zeronis

Zeronis Anti-Freeze, 1946 (SS) one-gallon can. $50-$75.

Canadian Imperial Quart Cans

Angelo Exploration Ltd.
Purity 99

Purity 99 Motor Oil, 1965 (SS) Imperial quart can, $35-$45 US; Purity 99 Outboard, 1960 (SS) Imperial quart can, $40-$60 US.

Beaver Oil Company
Windsor, Ontario

Beaver Heavy Duty, 1960 (SS) Imperial quart can. $25-$35 US.

Apco Petroleum Products Ltd.
Leaside, Toronto

Apco Penn, 1949 (SS) Imperial quart can. $40-$50 US.

British American Oil Company; Canadian Dist., Gulf Oil Canada
Toronto, Ontario

Pennzoil, 1940 (SS) Imperial quart can. $40-$60 US. Has owls on reverse.

Motorine, 1934 (SS) Imperial quart can, $50-$75 US; BA ATF Type F, 1967 (SS) Imperial quart can, $25-$35 US.

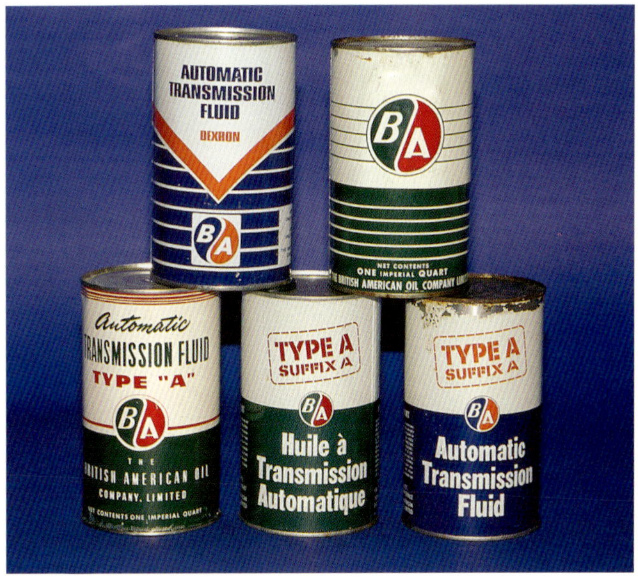

BA ATF/S-3 Diesel, 1952-1970 (SS) Imperial quart can. $35-$45 US.

All 1940-1952, (SS) Imperial quart cans. $40-$75 US.

BA DieseLube Heavy Duty, 1960 (SS) Imperial quart can. $40-$60 US.

BA Peerless/Heavy Duty, 1952-1967 (SS) Imperial quart can. $35-$45 US.

BA Frost Cop Anti-Freeze, 1960-1970 (SS) Imperial quart can. $35-$45 US.

BA Outboard/Utility Oil, 1960 (SS) Imperial quart can. $25-$35 US. This can has Outboard on one side and Utility on reverse.

1965-1970 (SS) Imperial quart can. $35-$45 US.

1970-1973 (SS) Super Duty (CP) Imperial quart can. $20-$30 US each.

Gulf Motor Oil, 1967 (SS) Imperial quart can. $25-$35 US.

BA Outboard Oil, 1961 (PB) Imperial quart can. $25-$40 US.

1970-1973 (SS) Imperial quart can. $20-$30 US each.

British Petroleum Oil Company
Montreal, Quebec

All 1965 (SS) Imperial quart can. $25-$35 US each.

BP Autogol, 1966 (SS) Imperial quart can. $25-$35 US.

BP AntiGel Anti Freeze, 1965 (SS) Imperial gallon can. $25-$35 US. Also sold in quart size.

Canadian Industrial Alcohol Company Ltd.
Montreal, Corbyville, Toronto, Winnipeg

Maple Leaf Anti Freeze, 1950 (SS) Imperial quart can. $45-$65 US.

Canadian Oil Company Ltd.
White Rose
Toronto, Ontario

Motor Oil, 1940 (SS) Imperial quart can, Anti-Freeze, 1940 (SS) Imperial quart can. $125-$225 US each.

National Motor Oil, 1950 (SS) Imperial quart can. $25-$35 US.

White Rose Outboard, 1961 (SS) Imperial quart can. $35-$45 US each.

White Rose Motor Oils, 1955-1961 (SS) Imperial quart can. $40-$75 US each.

White Rose Pressure Gun Grease, 1945 (SS) one-lb can. $50-$85 each.

White Rose Motor Oils, 1962 (SS) Imperial quart can. $40-$75 each.

Canadian Petro Fina Ltd.

Fina, 1960-1970 (SS) Imperial quart can. $25-$35 US each.

Fina Outboard, 1962 (SS) Imperial quart can. $25-$35 US.

Canadian Petroleum Co. Ltd.
Montreal, Quebec

Hot Penn, 1941 (SS) Imperial quart can. $40-$60 US.

Canadian Tire Corporation
Toronto, Ontario

Perma Fill Anti-Freeze, 1960 (SS) Imperial quart can. $50-$95 US.

J. I. Case
Toronto, Ontario

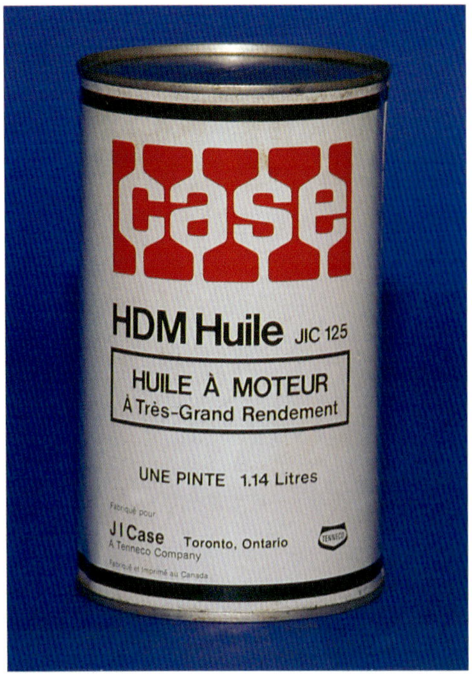

Case HDM, 1970 (SS) Imperial quart can. $20-$30 US.

Champlain Oil Products Limited
Monreal, Quebec

Champlain Citadel, 1947 (SS) Imperial quart can. $40-$60 US.

Chevron; Standard Oil of British Columbia; RPM

RPM, 1956-1970 (SS) Imperial quart can. $20-$30 US each.

RPM, 1956-1970 (SS) Imperial quart can. $20-$30 US each.

RPM, 1956-1970 (SS) Imperial quart can. $20-$30 US each.

Cities Service Canada Ltd.

Koolmotor, 1934 (SS) Imperial quart can. $35-$65 US.

Cities Service Outboard, 1955 (SS) Imperial quart can. $25-$35 US.

Cities Service Koolmotor, Cities Service Motor Oil, Cities Service "C" Series, 1956 (SS) Imperial quart can. $25-$35 US each.

Cities Service HD Koolmotor, Cities Service "C" Series, 1957 (SS) Imperial quart cans. $40-60 US each.

Cities Service Blue Club Motor Oil, 1963 (SS) 2-gallon can. $20-$40 US.

Cooperative Federal de Quebec; Federated Co-operatives Ltd.; Maritime Co-operatives Services; United Co-operatives of Ontario

Montreal; Saskatoon, Saskatchewan; Moncton, New Brunswick; Mississauga, Ontario

Co-op HD 7, 1970 (SS) Imperial quart can. $20-$30 US.

Imperial Esso

Toronto, Ontario

Imperial Polarine for Fords, 1925 (SS) Imperial gallon can. $275-$500 US.

IH Corporation

Hamilton, Ontario

IH Low Ash Engine Oil, 1969 (SS) Imperial quart can. $20-$30 US.

Imperial Kerosene Tractor Oil, 1925 (SS) five Imperial gallon can. $275-$500.

Imperial Polarine, 1925 (SS) five Imperial gallon call. $175-$375 US.

Imperial Esso/Imperial Oil Limited, 1946 (SS) Imperial quart cans. $40-$60 US.

Imperial Thresher Hard Oil, 1925 (SS) 25-pound can. $225-$425.

Imperial Esso, 1955-1960 (SS) Imperial quart cans. $25-$35 US.

Imperial Esso, 1946-1958 (SS) Imperial quart cans. $25-$35 US.

Imperial Polarine Cup Grease, 1925 (SS) 25-pound can. $75-$150 US.

Imperial Esso, 1969 (SS) Imperial quart can. $25-$50 US.

Imperial Esso Marvelube, 1960 (SS) one-quart can; Mineralube, 1960 (SS) one-quart can; Uniflo, 1936 (SS) one-quart can; Motor Oil, 1963 (SS) one-quart can; Extra, 1963 (SS) one-quart can; Essolube HDX, 1960 (SS) one-quart can. $25-$45 US each.

Esso Motor Oil, 1965 (SS) Imperial quart can. $25-$35 US.

Imperial Esso, 1969 (SS) Imperial quart cans. $25-$50 US.

Esso Aviation Oil, Left: 1961 (SS) one-quart can; Right: 1957 (SS) one-quart can. $75-$125 US each.

Esso-Rad Anti-Freeze, Top: 1945 (SS) Imperial gallon can; Left: 1954 (SS) Imperial gallon can; Right: 1960 (SS) Imperial gallon can, $35-$45 US each. Also sold in quart size.

Outboard, 1962 (PB) Imperial quart can. $15-$25 US.

Emergency Gasoline Can, 1920 (RS) Imperial gallon can. $75-$125 US.

Marvelube Waterproof Grease, 1950 (SS) one-pound can. $30-$50 US.

Esso Marvelube Grease, 1950 (SS) one-pound can, $25-$35 US; Frigol Refrigerant Oil, 1960 (SS) one-pint can, $40-$60 US.

Imperial Esso Utility Engine Oil, 1960 (SS) one-quart can. $35-$45 US.

Imperial Products Can, 1940 (SS) one-quart can, $35-$55 US. Marvelube Outboard, 1955 (SS) one-quart can, $35-$50.

Emergency Gasoline Can, 1920 (RS) Imperial gallon can. $75-$125 US.

Irving, All 1965 (SS) Imperial quart cans. $40-$75 US each.

Irving Velco/Velco Heavy Duty, 1955-1971 all (SS) Imperial quart can. $35-$65 US.

Irving Oil Company Ltd.
St. John, New Brunswick

Left: Pennlube, 1940 (SS) Imperial quart can; Right: Velco, 1940 (SS) Imperial quart can. $40-$75 US each.

Kendall Refining Co. of Canada
Toronto, Ontario

Kendall 2000 Mile, 1939 (SS) Imperial quart can. $40-$50 US.

Massey-Harris Company Ltd.
Toronto, Ontario

Cream Separator Oil, 1930 (SS) one-quart can. $75-$125 US.

North Penn Oil Company
Warren, PA

Mohawk, 1950 (SS) Imperial quart can. $40-$60 US.

Mobil Oil of Canada Ltd.

Mobil, 1940-1965 (SS) Imperial quart can. $25-$45 US each

North Star Oil Co. Ltd.
Winnepeg, Manitoba

William Penn Heavy Duty, Left: 1954 (SS) Imperial quart can; Right: 1956 (SS) Imperial quart can. $40-$75 US each.

William Penn, Left: 1956 (SS) Imperial quart can; Right: 1954 (SS) Imperial quart can; Frigidal Anti-Freeze, 1956 (SS) Imperial quart can. $50-$75 US each.

William Penn Cup Lubricant, 1949 (SS) five-pound can. $40-$60 US.

Pioneer Oil Company
Philadelphia PA

Pennsylvania Motor Oil Safety Lube, 1958 (SS) Imperial gallon can. $50-$75 US.

Royalite Oil Company Ltd.
Calgary, Alberta

Royalite MS, 1965 (SS) Imperial quart can. $45-$65 US.

Phillips 66;Pacific Petroleums Ltd.
Calgary, Alberta

Phillips 66 Motor Oil, 1958 (SS) Imperial quart can, $40-$60 US; Pacific 66 HDS, 1965 (SS) Imperial quart can, $25-$35 US.

Left: Hallmark 1967 (SS) Imperial quart can; Right: Motor Oil, 1967 (SS) Imperial quart can, $25-$35 US each.

Royalite Outboard, 1961 (SS) Imperial quart can. $25-$35 US.

Shell Canada Ltd.
Toronto, Ontario

Shell X100, 1952 (SS) Imperial quart can, $40-$60 US; Golden Shell, 1938 (SS) Imperial quart can, $75-$125 US; Silver Shell, 1938 (SS) Imperial quart can, $75-$125 US.

Sentry Auto Stores
Toronto

Sentry Motor Oil, 1950 (SS) Imperial quart can. $75-$150 US.

Shell cans, Top: 1956 (SS) Imperial quart can; Left: 1951 (SS) Imperial quart can; Right: 1956 (SS) Imperial quart can. $25-$35 US each.

Golden Shell, 1964 (CP); Rotella Oil, 1969 (SS); Shell X100, 1956 (SS); Shell Engine Conditioning Oil, 1956 (SS); Shellzone, Anti-Freeze, 1960 (SS), all Imperial quart cans. $25-$45 each US.

Shell cans, Top left: 1971 (CP), Top right: 1971 (CP), Bottom left: 1969 (SS), Middle: 1969 (SS), Bottom right: 1971 (CP) all Imperial quart cans. $25-$35 US each.

Shell cans, Left to right: 1960 (SS), 1960 (SS), 1960 (SS), 1963 (SS), all Imperial quart cans. $25-$35 US.

Aero Shell Fluid 4, 1960 (SS) Imperial quart can. $75-$125 US.

Shell cans, 1956-1976 (SS) all Imperial quart cans. $25-$35 US.

Aero Shell Oil, Left: 1957 (SS); Right: 1961 (SS) Imperial quart cans. $40-$60 US each.

Aero Shell 65/100, both 1963 (SS) Imperial quart cans. $40-$60 US each.

Shellzone Anti-Freeze, 1969 (SS) one-gallon can. $25-$45 US. Also sold in one-quart can.

Shell cans, Top: Hydraulic Oil, 1956 (SS); Left: Quick-Mix outboard, 1963 (SS); Right: Shell Rimula (S-3) 1961 (SS) all imperial quart cans. $25-$45 US each.

Sun Oil Canada Ltd.

Sunoco Motor Oil, Sunoco Dynalube Motor Oil, Left to right: 1946 (SS) 1956 (SS) Imperial quart cans. $40-$50 US each.

Shell Outboard, Left: 1970 (CP); Right: 1971 (CP) Imperial quart cans. $20-$30 US each.

Supertest Petroleum Company Ltd.
London, Ontario

Gold Standard, 1946 (SS) Imperial quart can, $70-$150 US; Super Duty, 1946 (SS) Imperial quart can, $70-$125 US.

Supertest cans, 1955-1973 (SS) Imperial quart can. $40-$75 US.

Supertest Anti-Freeze, 1966 (SS) one-quart can. $40-$60 US.

Supertest Snowmobile Oil, 1970 (PB) Imperial quart can. $35-$40 US.

Texaco Canada Ltd.; McColl Frontenac Oil Co. Ltd.
Toronto, Ontario

Top: 1955 (SS), Left: 1949 (SS), Right: 1953 (SS), all Imperial quart cans. $25-$35 US each.

Texaco cans, Top left: 4/62 (SS), Top right: 5/59 (SS), Lower left: 3/60 (SS), Middle: 3/60 (SS), Right: 1/59 (SS), all Imperial quart cans. $25-$35 US each

Texaco Havoline/Motor Oil, Top: 1971 (SS), Left: 2/63 (SS), Right: 2/63 (SS), all Imperial quart cans. $25-$35 each US.

Tidewater Oil Company;Veedol Oil Company Canada Limited

Montreal, Toronto, Regina; Montreal, Toronto, Winnipeg

Tidex, 1950 (SS) Imperial quart can. $40-$60 US.

1936-1970 (SS) Imperial quart can. $25-$50 US each.

Trinidad Lease Holds Canada Ltd.
Port Credit, Ontario

1960 (SS) Imperial quart can. $40-$50 US.

Resources

Trade publications for collectors:

Petroleum Collectibles Monthly
P.O. Box 556
LaGrange, OH 44050-0556
(440) 355-6608 FAX (440) 355-4955

Check the Oil
P.O. Box 937
Powell, OH 43065-0937
(614) 848-5038

Collectors Clubs:

Gulf Oil Historical Society
14306 East Yankee Road
Ottawa Lake, MI 49267
www.gulfhistory.org

Western Vintage Oil and Gas Collectors Club
c/o Mr. Dave Spyker
Site 7, RR #1, Box 64
Dewinton, Alberta, Canada T0L 0X0
(403) 995-0308

Buyer of oil cans and Sohio items:

W. Clark Miller
9944 Gardenside Drive
Waite Hill, OH 44094-6949
(440) 942-1079

Sources for cans, signs, pumps, etc.

Vic's Place
124 North 2nd
Gutherie, OK 73044
www.vicsplace.com

Ed Copelin
P.O. Box 181
Fairfield, ME 04937

Bibliography

Benjamin, Scott, and Wayne Henderson. *Gas Globes: Amoco to Mobil and Affiliates*. Atglen, Pennsylvania: Schiffer Publishing Ltd., 1999.

Benjamin, Scott, and Wayne Henderson. *Gas Globes: Pennzoil to Union and Affiliates*. Atglen, Pennsylvania: Schiffer Publishing Ltd., 1999.

Benjamin, Scott, and Wayne Henderson. *Oil Company Signs, A Collector's Guide*. Osceola, Wisconsin: Motor Books International, 1995.

Benjamin, Scott, and Wayne Henderson. *Sinclair Collectibles*. Atglen, Pennsylvania: Schiffer Publishing Ltd., 1997.

Benjamin, Scott, and Wayne Henderson. *Standard Oil Co., The First 125 Years*. Osceola, Wisconsin: Motor Books International, 1996.

Benjamin, Scott, and Wayne Henderson. *Texaco Collectors' Guide*, Osceola. Wisconsin: Motor Books International, 1997.

Henderson, Wayne, and Scott Benjamin. *Guide to Gasoline Logos*. LaGrange, Ohio, Marshall, North Carolina: PCM Publishing Co., 1997.

Love, Ed, Wayne Henderson, and W. Clark Miller. *1990 Edition-The Master List of United States Oil Containers*. Colorado Springs, Colorado: Gas House Publications, Division of Villa Publishing Syndicate, 1990.

Love, Ed. *The American Oil Can Encyclopedia*. Colorado Springs, Colorado: Villa Publishing Syndicate, 1991.

McIntyre, J. Sam. *The Esso Collectibles Handbook: Memorabilia from Standard Oil of New Jersey*. Atglen, Pennsylvania: Schiffer Publishing Ltd., 1998.

Miller, W. Clark and Sabra Sonewald. *An Unauthorized Guide to Collecting Sohio*. Atglen, Pennsylvania: Schiffer Publishing Ltd., 2000.

Miller, W. Clark and Sabra Sonewald. *Collecting Oil Cans*. Atglen, Pennsylvania: Schiffer Publishing Ltd., 2001.

Moncrief, David L. *Got A Drop of Oil, An Introduction and Price Guide to Small Oilers*. Gas City, New Jersey: L-W Book Sales, 1998.

Whitworth, Charles. *Gulf Oil Collectibles*. Atglen, Pennsylvania: Schiffer Publishing Ltd., 1998.